TRAINING GAMES

TRAINING GAMES

Everything You Need to Know about Using Games to Reinforce Learning

Susan El-Shamy

Routledge
Taylor & Francis Group

NEW YORK AND LONDON

First published in 2001 by Stylus Publishing, LLC.

Published in 2023 by Routledge
605 Third Avenue, New York, NY 10017
4 Park Square, Milton Park, Abingdon, Oxon OX14 4RN

Routledge is an imprint of the Taylor & Francis Group, an informa business.

© 2001 Taylor & Francis Group

Library of Congress Cataloging-in-Publication Data
El-Shamy, Susan.
    Training games : everything you need to know about using games to
  reinforce learning/Susan El-Shamy.
      p. cm.
    Includes bibliographical references.
    ISBN 1-57922-040-1 (pbk. : alk. paper)
      1. Employees—Training of. 2. Training. 3. Management games.
  4. Learning strategies. I. Title.

HF5549.5.T7 E425 2001
658.3'124—dc21   2001020468

ISBN: 9781579220402 (pbk)
ISBN: 9781003448228 (ebk)

DOI: 10.4324/9781003448228

*In memory of my father, Ben Syphers,
and his love of Ping Pong, his skill at Euchre,
and his patience with Candyland.*

CONTENTS

INTRODUCTION

Are you a player of games? I am. I've loved playing games as long as I can remember. Card games, board games, computer games—I've spent endless hours of my life enjoying them all. I noticed early on in life that I could tell a great deal about people by playing games with them. From siblings, to friends, to colleagues, to clients—there was a lot to be learned from playing games.

When I was a graduate student studying educational psychology and counseling and guidance, I discovered experiential learning games and they became a part of my game-playing repertoire. As a counselor, therapist, and educator, I used experiential games to help groups of people raise their awareness of issues and broaden their perspectives of the possibilities. I realized that careful reflection and skillful facilitation of game-playing behaviors was a powerful learning tool. I also used experiential games and activities to help individuals get in touch with their thoughts, feelings, and behaviors. I saw the power of games to act as metaphors, to mirror attitudes and behaviors used in the outside world into the world of the game at hand.

Then, I changed careers from the academic world of teaching and counseling to the business world of training and development. And one of the first and most exciting discoveries I made in the business world was a whole new realm of games and simulations. I learned to use games to help departments find better and quicker processes, to assist groups in finding ways to work together more effectively, and to help individuals prepare for international work assignments. But I also continued to use games to help individuals reflect on their own thoughts, feelings, and behaviors; to raise awareness and open up new possibilities. And that is both exciting and satisfying.

When the opportunity to write this book came along, I wanted to share my love of game playing and my interest in using games to facilitate learning along with my additional interest in watching the growth and development of training games within the training and development industry. So, I have tried to cover all three of these interests in this book, along with giving you as much practical, useful advice and steps-to-follow as I could.

Who is this book for? Anyone who uses or is considering the use of training games. If you are new to training games, this book will give you a good "lay of the land" and a detailed map for getting to and through your first facilitation of a training game. If you are a seasoned veteran, there is information inside on the classifying of training games, the new realm of e-games and various Web sites you might find useful. And wherever you lie on the continuum of new to seasoned trainer, there is an Ultimate Training Game Assessment form that you can use not only to assess games, but also to guide you in creating your own training games.

The book is divided into two basic parts. Part One looks at some of the bigger picture, theoretical aspects of training games: what is a training game, the benefits of using training games, how learning psychology supports the use of training games, and an overview of the most common types of training games. Part Two gives you practical, applicable information: how to choose and use, set up and conduct, debrief and assess training games. Part Two also provides examples and illustrations of designing and using training games, as well as guidelines for creating your own training games.

In the final chapter of Part Two, I've also included a resource list of commercially available games, books of games, books about training games, and my favorite game-related Web sites. With the rapid changes occurring in the realm of e-learning, I worry that many of my references to Web sites and e-learning games, and to the current trends in the training industry, will change before the book goes to press, but that is inevitable and should not affect content and references too drastically!

For those of you who like to read nonfiction the way I do—here and there and back again—the chapters are written so that they can be randomly accessed. Each chapter begins with a short, personal anecdote and ends with an "In a Nutshell" section that summarizes the chapter.

As I will discuss throughout the book, there is something universal about playing a game, something that appeals to us all. There is pleasure in the playing of a game. The pleasure comes from the high level of involvement, the interaction with other players, the competition that continues throughout the game, the building of skills, and increasing of competencies over time. All of these factors work together to make the learning fun. And that's good. The pleasure in the playing attracts people to the learning, keeps people learning, and reinforces that learning.

Games are not the answer to all that ails our training endeavors, but games are an excellent tool, an almost miraculous medium, to engage the learner and reinforce the learning. So come with me into the land of training games and take a look around. I'm sure you'll enjoy the journey and the learning along the way.

PART ONE

WHAT'S IN A GAME?

One long rainy summer of my Indiana childhood, my brother, sister, and I spent hours in our garage playing "office." With three enormous Indianapolis phone books set up on TV tables, two of us would play workers, while the other played boss giving us names to look up in the phone books. Poking our heads down into the phone books, turning pages rapidly, we would run our fingers down the rows of names until one of us would jump up shouting, "I got it! I got it!" The worker who was first to find five names got to play boss until someone else found five names. On and on we played, forgetting to see if it was still raining.

I

LET'S PLAY A GAME

HISTORY AND DEFINITIONS OF GAMES

Remember when you were a child looking for something to do on a long, boring afternoon? And some friend or sibling would make the suggestion, "I know, let's play a game!" If you were anything like I was, you would suddenly perk up, begin to inventory the possibilities, and feel reenergized by the fun and challenge that lay ahead. There is something about playing a game that appeals to us all, something universal that reaches across time and place and calls to the child within.

Everyone played games as a child. You did, didn't you? What were your favorite games? Outdoor games like *Hide and Seek, Kickball,* and *King of the Hill?* Rainy-day indoor games like *Sorry, Monopoly,*

Parcheesi, Clue, Chutes and Ladders? Or maybe you liked strategy games like *Connect Four, Battleship,* and *Mastermind?* What about video games? Did you ever play *Pac Man, Space Invaders, Qbert?* Which ones were you hooked on? Which ones carried your initials? Can you remember the day you got your first Nintendo, your first Gameboy?

The playing of games is not just a part of childhood; it's a part of life. What games do you still play? *Scrabble? Sequence? Pictionary?* How about *Touch Football, Horse,* or *Softball?* What about computer games? I'm not just talking *Myst* or *The Legend of Zelda,* what about *Solitaire* or *Free Cell?* Most of us play games, and watch games being played, throughout our lives, across cultures, and throughout time.

Ancient Egyptians enjoyed games. Pictures of games and game playing can still be seen on the walls of tombs and temples that are thousands of years old. The earliest known game board, measuring about 7 by 3 inches and dating from 4000 to 3500 B.C., was found in a predynastic cemetery in El-Mehasna, Egypt.[1] It appears to be similar to *Senet,* a backgammon-style game based on the underworld that was played in ancient Egypt for more than a thousand years.[2] One of the most enchanting treasures found in King Tut's tomb was an ivory and jewel-encrusted game board.

Variants of the popular African strategy game of *Mancala,* which uses a carved wooden game board and involves the moving of dried beans from pocket to pocket, have been found in East and West Africa, southern India, and Sri Lanka.[3] The game board used in *Chess* today is a descendant of a game board that originated in India some five thousand years ago.[4]

North American Indian tribes played games of chance and games of dexterity. Such games were for adults and sometimes young men and women, but never children. Children had many amusements, but games were serious endeavors usually played at fixed times for special occasions such as festivals and religious ceremonies.[5]

Although many ancient games were used in connection with religious rituals and celebrations, like those of the North American Indians, the majority of games played in Europe and North America up until the late eighteenth century was strictly for recreational purposes. Certain games, especially more physical, sporting-type games, may have helped to develop agility and dexterity useful to some occupations, but on the whole, games were not used as a means of instruction until the nineteenth century.

It was in the nineteenth century that popular European board games began to make their way across the Atlantic Ocean. Many Americans of this time period perceived games as superficial and time wasting at best, and as licentious works of the Devil at worst. Thus, when European recreational board games began arriving, they had to be modified into games of moral and educational instruction in order to appeal to the more puritanical tastes of the Americans. These became the first examples of what might be defined as "educational games" in America.

The *Mansion of Happiness,* the first board game produced in the United States, had the pedagogical purpose of teaching children the difference between good and bad.[6] *The Checkered Game of Life* had a moral motif involving happy old age versus a life of ruin.[7] Milton Bradley, the manufacturer, claimed that *The Checkered Game of Life* "inaugurated the introduction of moral and instructive games . . . and served to break down an unjust prejudice against all home amusements."[8] During this time, heavily didactic games on nature, literature, and scripture appeared and came into common use. To reassure wary parents who bought these games, many included literature and verses exhorting children to be good.[9]

The use of games for the training of adults was relatively unknown until the mid-nineteenth century when European military forces began using war games such as elaborate sandboxes with model soldiers and war exercises were carried out in the field.[10] Over time, war games and simulations became a common feature of military training; and, after World War II, business education programs in the United States began using similar simulations.

In the 1960s and 1970s, the human relations training movement and the growth and popularity of encounter groups brought an assortment of structured learning experiences and experiential exercises into various adult learning arenas.[11] Along with these experiential activities came a variety of games and some of the early "classic" simulations like *BaFá BaFá,* the timeless cross-cultural simulation designed by Garry Shirts.[12]

The 1980s brought a great increase in corporate training programs and training books; materials and games poured into the marketplace. *Games Trainers Play*[13] and *More Games Trainers Play*[14] appeared in the early 1980s, as did various other volumes of exercises, energizers, and training games. A great interest in work teams, particularly "self-directed," "high-performance" work teams, arose in the mid-1980s and a multitude of books and materials appeared to help working America build teams. Team-building games and activities staked out a large territory of the training and development marketplace and still hold their ground today.

The 1990s saw the birth of "corporate universities" and global corporate training programs. Business simulations prospered. *Still More Games Trainers Play* appeared in 1991[15] and corporate university bookstores filled their shelves with books, videos, CDROMs, and training games. Adventure training, outdoor learning, and other experiential group games and activities became popular. Computer-based training programs arrived on the scene and, gradually, they began to get used, particularly to teach computer skills. Simple games and quizzes were utilized in many of these early CDROM training packages, mostly to test and practice skills.

As the 1990s moved along, the prospect of "e-learning" grew, and pioneers of training and development explored new territories and wrote home of vast new regions of possibilities. But, it took the New Millennium to bring an explosion of "e-learning." Training programs went online and so did training games. Corporate universities meshed or melted into corporate "e-training" and new types of training games began to emerge—e-mail games and E-Sims. Then, Marc Prensky introduced *The Monkey Wrench Conspiracy*,[16] complete with Agent Moldy, and "digital game-based learning" took off. We'll look at all of these e-learning developments in Chapter 4; but right now, let's talk about games in general and why games have been such an integral part of the history of training and development and why they are carving out a significant portion of the present and future of e-learning.

What Is a Game?

What is there about playing a game that appeals to so many of us? Why have games proliferated throughout time and been a part of every world culture? Why do we love playing games? What keeps us going back for another round, another attempt at winning? Every game, from *Chess* to *Hide and Seek,* from *Old Maid* to *Grim Fandango,* from *BaFá BaFá* to *The Monkey Wrench Conspiracy,* is played in the context of an imaginary, closed world that is defined by given boundaries and nonnegotiable rules, where we all begin as equal players on an even playing field, with the same amount of time and resources to accomplish the mission, or achieve the goal and win. And that makes for exciting stuff!

Part of what makes a game so absorbing is that sense of being set apart from the rest of the given environment—being in "The Zone" as heavy-duty game players say. One of the definitions given by the *Random House Dictionary* for a game is "a competitive activity involving skill, chance, or endurance played according to rules."[17] The competitive nature of a game and the elements that involve skill, chance, or endurance are key to making a game a game; and they contribute greatly to that total absorption that can be experienced in playing a game. They also contribute to the appeal of playing again and again. Competition in a game can be among players and/or between the player(s) and the game. The perfecting of a skill, the increasing of your own competence, can be very motivating and very rewarding.

In the *Oxford History of Board Games,* David Parlett writes that a formal game has a twofold structure based on ends and means: "Ends. It is a contest to achieve an objective. . . . Only one of the contenders, be they individuals or teams, can achieve it, since achieving it ends the game. . . . Means. It has an agreed set of equipment and of procedural 'rules' by which the equipment is manipulated to produce a winning situation."[18]

So, according to Parlett, to be a game there must be an ends—an objective achieved through a contest—and there must be a means to do so—a playing context of equipment and rules.

It's interesting to note that in his book, Parlett attempts to draw a distinction between games and sports but finds it almost impossible to do. Indoor versus outdoors doesn't work, nor does physical versus nonphysical, although it begins to separate the two. There are not many games that are very physical, and most sports are fairly physical, but then what is billiards or pool? Many sports have professional ranks as well as amateur, but then there are professional chess players, even professional miniature golf players. However, for the most part, in this book, we will be looking at training games and there is yet to be a professional versus amateur distinction among the players of training games! Although with some of the new e-games and digital game-based learning, that could just be a matter of time.

If we combine the definitions from the dictionary and David Parlett, we have the following: a competitive activity involving skill, chance, or endurance between individuals or teams to achieve an objective within a given context of equipment and rules. Not a bad definition, but not quite there yet.

What are the factors that make a game a game and not just an activity or a pastime? An activity is anything we do that occupies our time. A pastime is anything we do that makes the time pass agreeably. A game, however, does much more than just occupy our time or make time pass by agreeably. A really good game almost seems to transcend time and place by absorbing us completely. The phenomenon of total absorption that can give the quality of "other worldliness" to a game is missing from the definition. Although the word "context" means the circumstances that surround an event and certainly the circumstances that surround any game include rules, equipment, time factors, even a story line or fantasy element.

Maybe it is the combination of the components of a game working together that brings about the sense of "being in another world." And it is the unique combination of "meeting a challenge" in an "imaginary world" that strikes our fancy and makes games so appealing. Let's hold off on a final definition of "game" until we explore the world of training games and see if we can gain further insight there.

What Is a Training Game?

Training games fall within a broad category of learning techniques commonly labeled "interactive learning activities." These are activities in which "participants interact with one another for the purpose of learning something."[19] This category of interactive learning techniques includes such things as discussions, activities, exercises, role-plays, games, and simulations.

Today, the number of interactive learning approaches being used and marketed in the field of adult education and training is growing at an unprecedented rate. Along with this growth has come a problem of terminology that has become more and more muddled as products proliferate. The term "game" is often used interchangeably with activity, or the two are used together, as in "team development games and activities."

One of the problems in defining the phrase "training game" is the inconsistent use of many of these interactive learning terms, particularly the terms "activity," "game," and "simulation." These three words are sometimes used interchangeably, plus there is a category of games that is called "simulation-games," which adds even more to the confusion. Therefore, much of what you read in the training and development literature and in books on training games is not specifically directed toward games per se, but toward games and activities in general, and, in an even broader sense, toward interactive learning approaches.

This can be disconcerting to the person shopping for an interactive training game. Some experts in the field suggest that the "mislabeling" is caused by categorizing activities according to surface characteristics; others attribute mislabeling to the packaging and marketing of learning products with what will sell foremost in mind. It's interesting to note that in the original 1980 edition of *Games Trainers Play*,[20] a book that is often considered the first real book of training games, many of the games were not games at all in the strict sense of defining a game.

You may also find the word "experiential" used in the same way as the word "interactive." In general, when it comes to nonelectronic training games, "Interactive learning can be regarded as a wide range of activities in which participants in an event interact with each other for the purposes of education and training."[21] Experiential learning is often used to indicate that the major learning has occurred from the learner's physical experiencing of something, rather than the learner's interaction with content material. At times you will find the two terms used interchangeably, and, sometimes, they will appear together as in "interactive, experiential training." Suffice it to warn those new to the world of training games, that it is a bit messy out there!

I will not even go into the various definitions of training vs. learning vs. professional development. For the most part, I will be using the term "learning" in the most general sense, the term "training" in the more specific sense of learning that takes place in regard to work or to specific skill development, and "professional development" most specifically as something done to stay up-to-date or to rise within one's profession.

Let's discuss the concepts of game and training game a bit further. We have already touched on some of the basic factors that make a game a game—a competitive activity involving skill, chance, or endurance between individuals or teams to achieve an objective within a given context of equipment and rules. When it comes to using games in education and training, the same aspects of a game hold true, with the additional factor that the skills being built and the competencies being developed are specifically related to learning objectives and the content of the course, workshop, seminar, or learning activity.

Margaret Gredler in her book, *Designing and Evaluating Games and Simulations,* writes that, "Classroom games may be used for any of four general academic purposes. They are (1) to practice and/or refine knowledge/skills already acquired; (2) to identify gaps or weaknesses in knowledge/skills; (3) to serve as a summation or review; and (4) to develop new relationships among concepts and/or principles."[22] And, as we will see in Chapter 3 of this book, most of the training games on the market today fall within these four academic purposes.

Let's investigate the various factors present in a game and consider their impact on learning, since learning is the ultimate goal of a training game. Again, the factors are:

- A competitive activity between individuals or teams
- Within a given context of equipment and rules
- Meeting a challenge involving skill, chance, or endurance
- To achieve an objective

Players Competing

In his book, *Simulations,* Ken Jones writes, "Whatever the motive for running a game (enjoyment, education, or competition) all the participants are in one basic role—players."[23] A referee is not a player in the game, nor is the coach; and in the case of training games, nor is the instructor or facilitator. Players are those actually playing the game, and they begin the game on an equal basis. Occasionally, players may have different roles, names, or assignments, such as the "banker" in *Monopoly*, but they all start at "Go" and are subject to the same points and penalties throughout the game. In a simulation, however, the players may not begin the activity on an equal basis. Many simulations are deliberately set up so that participants do not start equally nor receive equal treatment. This is one of the factors that separate games and simulations.

The use of competition in a learning setting is not always seen as desirable. And certainly the misuse of competition should be of great concern to trainers and facilitators of games. A game should never be designed or facilitated in such a way that it focuses on competition and winning above and beyond all else. We have all experienced "a little friendly competition" at some point in our lives that turned out to be anything but friendly. Undoubtedly, you will encounter participants who have had such experiences and now balk at the suggestion of playing a game. Ken Jones asserts, "People who don't like playing games because they do not like competition are really asking for security, kindness and professionalism."[24] And the effective facilitator provides these, as we shall discuss in Chapter 5.

Players may not always be equal in skill levels. Some games may adjust for this by giving a "handicap." Other games may have different tiers of competition: beginners, intermediates, or advanced. And sometimes, players themselves may adjust for skill levels within the "unwritten rules" of the game by aiding the new player with an extra turn, or a little help along the way. But in general, players should be at an equal level of ability, with the same amount of time and resources to accomplish the mission.

Within a Given Context

The phrase, "play a game" is interesting. We do not "do a game" or "perform a game," we play a game. The word play when used as a verb has the double connotation of "acting," as in enacting or impersonating, and of "competing," as in contending or opposing. Both of these meanings come into play when playing a game. Jones stresses that, "There must be consciousness of a closed environment, an unreal world which completely justifies the behaviour. . . ."[25] Gredler writes, ". . . it is important to remember that any game is a fantasy world, defined by its particular rules and efforts to win within those rules."[26]

The circumstances that surround any game include rules, equipment, time factors, and story line or fantasy element. The imaginary world—story line or fantasy element—of any given game may or may not be fully described. It can be as simple as "pretend you're in an office" or as complex as the richly embellished, multileveled, technicolor world of a computer game. The closed environment of a game can even be entirely unstated, as it often is in card games or simple paper-and-pencil games. But the notion that game playing is a world apart, where behaviors follow the rules and where outcomes are not necessarily those that would happen in real life, is accepted by all.

The fantasy aspect of games is often overlooked or brushed aside when it comes to training games, but it can be a very important factor in the overall success of a training game. A game can act as a metaphor and players will project their attitudes and behaviors from real life into the imaginary world of the game. Such projection, when recognized and explored, can offer important learning opportunities. Games can offer individuals a glimpse into their habits, their routines, and their tendencies to think, feel, and behave in certain ways.

As we will see in Chapter 3, many simple paper-and-pencil training games make almost no use of fantasy and are still quite successful. Perhaps the rules and time limits are enough to give such games the feel of being "set apart." But the simple addition of a story line or the use of phrases like, "Pretend you are members of a search team," can trigger emotions and elevate the simplest of training games to new heights of involvement.

In her book *Tales for Trainers,* Margaret Parkin discusses the use of stories and metaphors to facilitate learning; she writes, ". . . the more the content activates the imagination, through the inclusion of novel situations, fantastic creatures or mythical beings, and stirs the emotions—humour, pathos, empathy—the more likely the message is to be remembered."[27] I think the same holds true with games to some degree. When you are imagining yourself stranded in the Himalayas and knowing you must work well with other team members in order to survive, that image and those circumstances will help you remember the skills it takes to get groups to work together.

A different aspect of using story telling in games is that of having players tell stories as part of the playing. There are games that require the players to either relate personal experiences or make up stories within the context of the game. Such activities can add involving emotional elements to a game. Joshua Kerievsky of Industrial Logic combines card game playing and story telling in his game, *Patterns Poker,*[28] which adds an involving, emotional element to the learning experience and a feeling of being "set apart" as players tell stories about their experiences.

The rules and regulations in our imaginary world of games are always described, usually quite thoroughly so; and the players must try to win in conformity to the set of rules. There is often a time limit given in the rules. But Ken Jones writes that games "also have 'a spirit of the rule'—an unwritten code covering a wide range of actions which are not banned by the rules, but are generally regarded as unsporting."[29] These unwritten rules of fair play and acceptable behavior must also be followed by the players if the game is to be successful. At times, the facilitator may have to enforce these unwritten rules as well as the written ones.

Another of the distinctions that is made between games and simulations has to do with this notion of being a world apart where results are not necessarily those that would happen in real life. In a game, you do not always behave as you would in real life; you use whatever behaviors are allowed by the rules, both written and unwritten. That is, while you wouldn't physically harm or degrade another player, you might trick them by finding a way to do something within the rules that, outside the game, you would never do. Jones explains, "Games do not have real-world ethics whereas simulations usually include real-world ethics. . . . A well-designed simulation provides enough key facts to allow the participants to function professionally."[30] In fact, the point of a simulation is to have the learner practice dealing with situations just as they would in real life. Therefore a simulation is not a game.

Meeting a Challenge

For a game to be involving and motivating, there must be some challenge to it. It cannot be won too easily. Skill, chance, and endurance are elements that provide challenge. Most training games have at least some element of chance involved, for instance, the roll of the dice, the hand you are dealt, and the obstacles you encounter. However, many interactive training designers feel that the element of chance should be minimized in training games. ". . . Academic games should avoid dependence on luck, chance or random search strategies in order to win . . ." advises Gredler.[31]

Endurance often comes into play, not only in physical games, but also in games that take a lot of time and mental energy. Indeed, the endurance factor can become critical to the effectiveness of a game. How many times have you stopped a game before it was finished because you ran out of time or became mentally or physically exhausted? It is important that a training game not become an endurance contest. In training games, skill development should be the chief factor providing the challenge. And when you think about it, isn't skill development the key factor that keeps us playing any game over and over? It is very rewarding to observe yourself getting better and better at doing some difficult task. The reinforcement of experiencing skill building can be very powerful.

To Achieve an Objective

One final aspect of game playing that needs to be examined is that of achieving an objective. This usually entails keeping score or measuring accomplishments with an established agreement of what it takes to win. The whole concept of competing implies measurement of some sort and knowing what constitutes winning.

One of the first questions raised while exploring a new game is, "How do you win?" This is an important question as players begin a game and the answer is not always self-evident. Have you ever tried to explain American *Football* to someone from the United Kingdom or seen someone from the United Kingdom trying to explain *Cricket* to an American? As players play and try to win, a scoring mechanism must be provided to enable them to monitor their progress and to ascertain winners and losers. And it must be easily understood by all.[32] The goal of any training game must be measurable and evident to everyone. It should be clearly stated and understood by every player before play begins.

The mission of a game is connected to the context or "the world" that has been created to play the game. It can be as simple as moving your pawn from square to square around the *Candyland* game board or as complex as getting Mario or Luigi through the various obstacles in eight different worlds. The mission is the "what you must do" of the game: catch the football and run toward the goal post of your opponent, move around the board buying properties and buildings and paying rents and fines, or find a beepless path across the carpet maze. The goal, however, tells you what is considered a win: "be the first person to land on home," "have the most points when time runs out," or "be the first group to complete all four sections of the puzzle and return to the classroom."

As was stated earlier, training games differ from other games in regard to their purpose and the concept of winning. As Gredler explains, "First, they require specific knowledge in a defined subject area or discipline . . . second, the intellectual skills required in the game are those that are applicable beyond the game itself to the particular course content."[33]

The term "business game" is sometimes used with training games and simulations that require trainees to gather information, analyze that information, and make decisions. Such business games are used primarily for management skill development. These games stimulate learning because participants are actively involved and they mimic the competitive nature of business.[34]

Definitions

And so, what is a game? By including all of the important components that we have just reviewed and making a few adjustments here and there, the definition of a game that we will be using in this book is as follows:

> A game is a competitive activity played according to rules within a given context, where players meet a challenge in their attempt to accomplish a goal and win.

And a training game is defined as:

> A training game is a competitive activity played according to rules within a given context, where players meet a challenge in their attempt to accomplish a goal and win, and, in which the skills required and competencies being built in the game are those that are applicable beyond the game itself to the particular subject matter being studied.

When in doubt as to whether to classify a training exercise as a game or an activity, check for the key components. Does it look like a game? Are there players competing to win? Is there a challenge involved as players follow rules to accomplish a measurable goal? Does it sound like a game? Are players enthusiastically engaged? Are they energized and into a world of their own within the game? If it looks like a game and sounds like a game and has all the components of a game, it probably is a game!

In a Nutshell

There is something universal about playing a game, something that appeals to us all. Games are played in all cultures and have existed throughout time. We all played games in our childhood and continue to play games and watch games being played throughout our lives. The use of games for the training of adults was relatively unknown until the mid-nineteenth century when European military forces began using war games. Slowly the use of training games moved from the military into business and industry, and by the 1960s and then into the 1970s and 1980s, training games became an accepted and utilized training tool in training and development programs.

To define a game requires combining the competitive elements that involve a challenge to meet a goal with the contextual elements provided by rules, equipment, time factors, and story or fantasy. To define a training game is difficult due to the inconsistent use of many interactive learning terms, particularly the terms "activity," "game," and "simulation." In general, however, the basic definition of a game holds true for a training game with the additional factor that the skills being built and the competencies being developed in a training game are specifically related to learning objectives and the content of a course, workshop, seminar, or learning activity.

In conclusion, we have defined a game as *a competitive activity played according to rules within a given context, where players meet a challenge in their attempt to accomplish a goal and win.* And a training game is *a competitive activity played according to rules within a given context, where players meet a challenge in their attempt to accomplish a goal and win, and, in which the skills required and competencies being built in the game are those that are applicable beyond the game itself to the particular subject matter being studied.*

Notes

1. Matthew J. Costello, *The Greatest Games of All Times* (New York: John Wiley and Sons, 1991).

2. Ibid.

3. Ibid.

4. Marvin Kaye, *The Story of Monopoly, Silly Putty, Bingo, Twister, Frisbee, Scrabble, Et Cetera* (New York: Stein and Day, 1973).

5. Stewart Culin, *Games of the North American Indians* (New York: Dover Publications, 1975).

6. Brian Love, *Great Board Games* (New York: MacMillan Publishing Co. 1979).

7. Ibid.

8. Ibid.

9. Marvin Kaye, *The Story of Monopoly.*

10. Elyssebeth Leigh, and Jeff Kinder, *Learning through Fun and Games* (Australia: McGraw Hill, 1999).

11. Ibid.

12. Garry Shirts, *BaFá BaFá Simulation Training Systems,* Del Mar, CA.

13. Edward Scannell, and John Newstrom, *More Games Trainers Play* (New York: McGraw-Hill, 1983).

14. Ibid.

15. Edward Scannell, and John Newstrom, *Still More Games Trainers Play* (New York: McGraw-Hill, 1991).

16. Marc Prensky, *The Monkey Wrench Conspiracy* (New York: Games2Train, 2000).

17. *Random House Dictionary* (New York: Random House, Inc., 1988).

18. David Parlett, *The Oxford History of Board Games* (London: Oxford University Press, 1999).

19. Ken Jones, *Simulations: A Handbook for Teachers and Trainers* (London: Kogan-Page, 1995).

20. John Newstrom, and Edward Scannell, *Games Trainers Play* (New York: McGraw-Hill, 1980).

21. Ken Jones, *Simulations.*

22. Margaret Gredler, *Designing and Evaluating Games and Simulations* (Houston, TX: Gulf Publishing, 1994).

23. Ken Jones, *Simulations.*

24. Ibid.

25. Ibid.

26. Margaret Gredler, *Designing and Evaluating Games and Simulations.*

27. Margaret Parkin, *Tales for Trainers* (London: Kogan Page, 1998). (Distributed in the United States by Stylus Publishing.)

28. Joshua Kerievsky, *Design Patterns Playing Cards* (San Francisco, CA: Industrial Logic, 2000).

29. Ken Jones, *Simulations.*

30. Ibid.

31. Margaret Gredler, *Designing and Evaluating Games and Simulations.*

32. Ken Jones, *Simulations.*

33. Margaret Gredler, *Designing and Evaluating Games and Simulations.*

34. Raymond A. Noe, *Employee Training and Development* (New York: McGraw-Hill, 1999).

I remember years ago watching my younger daughter sitting cross-legged in front of the TV set, totally engrossed as she played a Super Mario Brothers game on her Nintendo. After a few minutes it became apparent to me that she wasn't trying to win. In fact, she was deliberately letting all those extra lives expire as she searched for hidden objects, discovered secret passages, and built her flying skills. When I asked about her behavior, she sighed and replied, "Mom, there's more to playing than winning. Sometimes you gotta lose a little to learn a lot."

2

IT'S NOT WHETHER YOU WIN OR LOSE

LEARNING THEORY AND TRAINING GAMES

With so many engaging elements that make a game a game, it is easy to see why games make such an excellent vehicle for learning. Two elements in particular stand out—*competition* and *pleasure*. Everyone likes to play a game. Everyone likes to win. But there's more to a good game than winning. There is *pleasure in the playing*. The pleasure comes from the high level of involvement, the interaction with other players, the competition that continues throughout the game, the building of skills and increasing of competencies over time. All of these factors work together to make the learning fun. And that's good. The pleasure in the playing attracts people to the learning, keeps people learning, and reinforces that learning.

Along with the pleasure in the playing, there are other unique benefits that games can bring to your training programs. The various aspects of these benefits will be discussed in this chapter and throughout the book, but right now, maybe just to whet your interest, I want to share with you my own Top Ten Reasons for Training with Games.

Susan's Top Ten Reasons for Training with Games

1. Games Are Fun

Games provide an element of fun and excitement to training programs. They can be totally engaging. Games generate enthusiasm through meaningful challenge, involvement, and motivation to reach a goal. Games are relaxing; they can counteract stress and worry about learning. Games can make learning enjoyable, even when there is little interest in the material. The pleasure in the playing of the game spills over into the entire training event.

2. Games Are Dynamic

Games are dynamic; they involve movement and continual change. They can relate to many issues and topics at the same time and have many things happening at the same time. Games include surprise, conflict, and challenge. Games bring art, drama, color, sound, movement; they engage our senses. An upbeat, fast-paced game can provide a change of pace, a change in tempo, a change in mood, a change in attitude.

3. Games Provide a Safe Arena for Practice

Games can provide repetition and reinforcement of key information and give feedback. Game players can make mistakes and learn from those mistakes. Players can safely fail and try again. The safety and structure provided by the rules and boundaries of the imaginary world of a game are conducive to testing out new knowledge, exploring different ideas, identifying weaknesses, and practicing new behaviors. Within the context of a game, players are more open to trying out new ideas and behaviors. "It's just a game. Try it."

4. Games Make the Learning Concrete

Games take information that has been talked about and allow participants to do something with it. Games can immerse players in realistic, complex experiences. Players can increase their understanding of new concepts; they can use new knowledge, try out new behaviors, and apply new ideas. Linking action to information is important. Making learning concrete during the training will increase the chances of it being used after the training is over.

5. Games Let the Learning Sink In

Games can provide a medium for further examination, analysis, and interpretation of new material. Opportunities for meaningful discussion and extensive dialogue can be built into games. Players can play with the ideas, concepts, and behaviors explored in the training. And, this can be done in an involving and exciting manner.

6. Games Encourage Socializing

Games let you be social. Have you ever been in a class where there were other people that you would have liked to have met and interacted with, but you didn't get the chance? Games allow for mixing, mingling, and meeting others. This also means hearing the opinions of others, discussing content with others, and having others reinforce the learning. A good trainer will make sure that socializing happens. A good game just increases those chances!

7. Games Can Level the Playing Field

Sometimes there are noticeable differences in status, experience, and/or knowledge among participants. Games can level the playing field a bit. The rules apply to all players and everyone has a chance to win. A game makes the players equals among equals, or at least equals among not so equals.

8. Games Let the Trainer Monitor the Learning

While the participants are playing the game, the trainer can watch them play, observe how well they are doing with the course content, and listen in on their comments and criticisms. You can find out if they are "getting it," or whether you need to repeat or reinforce something. A game can let you know if it is all right to continue.

9. Games Make Training More Appealing

Because games are fun, they can lessen the bad reputation that training sometimes has. For people who have been forced to suffer through dull, dreary training, with endless tell, tell, tell punctuated with an occasional test, finding a training program that includes the pleasant involving nature of a game can be a welcomed surprise and a tremendous relief. The more participants who experience learning that is pleasurable, the better it is for all of training in general.

10. Games Allow the Trainer a Time Out

Games let the trainer take a break from the spotlight and put the spotlight on the learners. After all, it is their show, not yours. You introduce and set up the game, and then you go "off stage" for a while. Even though you need to monitor the game, you can do that from the sidelines, sitting down, leaning back, sipping a soda. This more passive role allows you to relax and reenergize for the debriefing that will follow, but it also allows participants to take active responsibility for the learning that occurs during the game.

As you see from this Top Ten, and will continue to see throughout the book, training games have many benefits and are an ideal vehicle for learning. Yet, with all of these benefits and advantages, there can still remain a reluctance to jump on board. This reluctance may have much to do with the connotations of the phrase "play a game."

Ken Jones warns that, "The words game and play are high risk words in education and should be used with care."[1] And he's right. When some people hear the phrase "learning game" or "training game," they think "silly, foolish and time-wasting." Such associations lead to misconceptions about training games and, in turn, make some people reluctant to use games in their training for fear of being labeled "unprofessional."

This may be particularly true of people over the age of forty who were less exposed to "learning games" in their early educational experiences. Baby Boomers who grew up with Captain Kangaroo and played *Pong* in their twenties may be much less accepting of learning games than members of the "Nintendo" or "Net generation" who grew up with *Seasame Street* and played video games in their preteens or earlier.

Stop and think for a moment about your own learning experiences. What have you learned from playing games, all types of games? Did "learning games" play an important role in your early education? Did you sing along with Big Bird or Kermit to learn your alphabet? Did you learn to count with "the Count"? Did you sharpen your problem-solving skills getting through the third level of the Second World on *Super Mario Brothers II?* If you answered "no" to most of these questions, then you may be among the trainers and educators who did not have significant learning game and video game exposure in their early childhood. And this could contribute to a hesitation to use training games. It could also be that early learning experiences and beliefs about work, play, and learning get in the way of accepting the use of training games. Let's reevaluate some of those beliefs.

Learning—even learning about very serious issues, complex problems, and intricate procedures—does not have to be slow, quiet, dull, boring, or arduous. The same can also be said about work. Work is something that requires exertion or effort. But exerting yourself, putting out effort, does not have to be a boring or painful process. It is possible to enjoy work and it is possible to enjoy learning. What is even more to the point is that it is possible to enjoy learning even if the content of the learning is not interesting, in and of itself. Training games are a context that can make almost any learning material, at best, interesting and engaging, and at least, not dull or boring.

Also to be considered is the fact that "game playing" does not necessarily mean silly or trivial. It is possible to play a game that is fun without being frivolous. It is possible to play a game that is both enjoyable and instructive. Learning does not have to be painful, nor does it have to be pleasurable. But if I get a choice between the two, I'll go for pleasure. If it is possible to make learning fun, involving, absorbing, and interesting, why not do so?

Some people defend their reluctance to use games with concerns about the competitive factor in games. And certainly, the competitive element has to be managed carefully so that it does not overshadow the learning or cut into the fun. But, when the competition is designed into the game appropriately and the game is delivered correctly, competition becomes a plus for learning.

There is also the connotation that "games are for children" to be contended with, although this belief is diminishing with time. Certainly the adult game market, and I'm not talking X-rated here, is a huge market offering everything from "family tabletop" games to an incredibly vast array of computer and video games aimed specifically to players in their teens and twenties and beyond. Games can engage and motivate learners of any age. Moreover, reaching learners of all ages is becoming a key factor in training and development. At the same time that the workplace is struggling with constant change, technological advancement, and the need for continuous learning and knowledge management, it is also being filled with younger and younger workers.

The Baby Boomer majority in the world of work is moving over for the Nintendo Generation. This fresh generation has a whole new set of learning styles and learning expectations. They've grown up with electronic technology and are accustomed to a quick, sharp, concise presentation of information. The days of dry lectures, droning instructors, and filling out pages in a workbook are long gone. Today's trainees are pressed for time and hungry for information and skills. It is essential that today's trainers provide immediate access to the information and skills needed in the most engaging manner possible, and games are a great way to do that.

Maybe an interesting point to make here is the growing difference in age between those designing and delivering training and those being trained. Or at least between trainees and the people making decisions about training content, design, and delivery. Since over half of today's workers are under thirty-nine, they may be quite comfortable with training games, particularly electronic training games, but older managers and decision makers may need some gentle persuasion. And trainers of a certain age may need to raise their own comfort levels with game playing. Training games need to be pleasurable for both players and trainers!

In his book, *Digital Game-Based Learning,* Marc Prensky refers to the training being designed and delivered by members of the Baby Boom generation as "training that's happening in Pleasantville."[2] He suggests that the slow, step-by-step, text-oriented, tell-test style of Pleasantville will have a hard time winning the interest of younger trainees who have developed "hypertext" learning styles accustomed to speed, random access, graphics, and immediate pay-off.[3]

Perhaps the first steps out of training in Pleasantville can be paved with training games. There are mounds of learning research, as well as years of practical experience, that endorse games as an excellent learning tool. But every trainer who chooses to use games in his or her training programs should be prepared to defend that choice—for the next few years anyway. So, consider the rest of this chapter as providing ammunition to have handy for future occasions when someone starts taking "pot shots" at training games.

Whether you are trying to convince yourself or someone else that games are an appropriate tool for learning, it helps to be familiar with current learning theories. Indeed, to get the most out of the benefits of using training games, you must be well grounded in learning theory. So, I've done some homework for you and put together a list of basic learning criteria for training games. Then, I've listed some of the more popular learning theories found today with comments on each regarding their application to training games. I've also coded the learning theories to the training game criteria and at the end of the chapter present a matrix that illustrates which theories support which criteria.

The first six of my Top Ten Reasons for Training with Games are supported by current learning theory and are addressed within the ten learning criteria we will be looking at. The remaining four reasons for using training games have more to do with managing the training and will be addressed elsewhere in the book.

Some Basic Learning Criteria for Training Games
While it may not be possible for all training games to contain all of the following characteristics, and while it is also possible for some really dull, dumb games to contain many of these characteristics, in general,

a training game that is well designed and effective as a game will be even more effective as a learning tool if it does a number of the following:

1. Repeats and reinforces key information
2. Gives immediate feedback
3. Provides safe practice of new skills
4. Develops understanding of new concepts
5. Provides meaningful challenge
6. Stimulates as many senses as possible
7. Promotes extensive dialogue and discussion
8. Furnishes social contact and group work
9. Provides realistic, complex experiences
10. Includes analysis, interpretation, reflection

These learning criteria are all supported by a variety of learning theories. The more of these criteria that are met in training games, all other things being equal, the more effective those training games will be in regard to reinforcing learning. So, let's get started with the learning theories, which are presented in alphabetical order. Reference to the various criteria above will be made for each theory in parentheses following the name of each theory.

Accelerated Learning (6)

Proponents of accelerated learning theory say that "People process thought, communicate, learn, and remember through use of the five senses: visual, auditory, kinesthetic, olfactory, and gustatory and each of us tends to have one preferred sense. The most common being visual, auditory and kinesthetic."[4] What this means to learning is that different individuals will respond to different stimuli.

Many of the methods and techniques of accelerated learning have been incorporated into standard teaching and training approaches. For many years, Dave Meier and the Center for Accelerated Learning in Lake Geneva, Wisconsin, have done an excellent job of supporting and exhorting the use of accelerated learning methods "to involve participants in the learning process and overcome negative views toward learning itself or toward their own ability to learn."[5]

Among the many strategies and techniques of accelerated learning, the use of learning games is one of the most appealing and effective. The skillful use of a learning game can present a variety of stimuli touching on at least the three most common preferred senses. In a board game, for example, the visual aspects could include players looking at the board and the illustrations and instructions written on the board, watching the movement of the pawns around the board, and reading the information on cards that they draw. The kinesthetic aspects of a board game could include the feel of the cards when players shuffle them, draw them, and place them on the board and the feel of the pawns that are moved around the board.

Auditory aspects could include listening as players read their cards out loud and discuss card content among themselves and the sound of the cards being shuffled and the pawns clicking along the game board. I have even had players keep score with scented markers to add a bit of olfactory interest to a game. And, to go for the gustatory, a bit of chocolate as a reward here and there doesn't hurt either!

Adult Learning Theory (5,8,9)

The number of adult learners has grown immensely over the past twenty years; and, proportionately, the amount of interest, research, and writing in regard to this huge population of learners has grown as well. Susan Imel, education professor at Ohio State University, writes, "Adult learning is a huge enterprise, with activities exceeding the combined total of those taking place in elementary, secondary, and postsecondary institutions. Adults learn in a multitude of settings such as the home, the workplace, and community agencies, and for a variety of reasons—personal development, increased job knowledge, and community problem solving."[6]

When Malcolm Knowles, the great scholar-practitioner of adult learning, published *The Adult Learner* in 1973, he identified a number of important characteristics of adult learners.[7] These characteristics remain central to adult learning theory today. Knowles stressed that adult learners are usually quite practical, goal-oriented, and relevancy-oriented. For those of us who teach and train adults, this is constantly evident in the classroom. Participants in our classes want to know how playing a game will be useful to them, as well as how what they learn in a game is relevant to their work and their lives. For this reason, it is very important when introducing and debriefing a game, to explicitly link the learning to training goals and to the needs and concerns of your participants in the real world.

Knowles also described adult learners as autonomous and self-directed learners. Adults don't want to be lectured at and inundated with data. They want to be actively involved in their own learning process and training games can provide this. The adults in your training programs are there to be guided through a learning process that gives them useful information that they can apply immediately to help them with their work and their lives. Having fun doing so, is icing on the cake!

Perhaps the most important factor in ensuring that learning occurs in your programs and activities is motivation. In an ideal world, participants would show up for your training programs, eager, excited, highly motivated and ready to learn. In reality, some participants arrive open, expectant, and ready to learn and others arrive tired, turned off, and highly motivated to get out early. Our biggest challenge as teachers and trainers is to get each and every one of our participants engaged in learning, and games can be a great way to meet that challenge.

Adult learning theorists suggest a number of factors that serve as sources of motivation for adult learners, such as fulfilling external expectations, personal advancement, and the need for social relationships. Other sources of motivation are that of escape and stimulation. Attending training is often a welcomed break from the daily routine of the workplace. It "can relieve boredom and provide a contrast with the exacting details of life."[8] Among all the possible interactive learning activities provided in training, games often do the best job of providing escape and stimulation.

Brain-Based Learning (1,2,3,5,9)

Increasingly, educators are relying on brain-based learning theory, which is taking advantage of the growing body of evidence that neurologists are uncovering about how humans learn. Attention is being given in brain-based learning theory to how the human brain processes memory, emotion, attention, and patterning, among other areas of research.[9] The brain is described as a parallel processor that performs several activities at once. Effective learning is seen as engaging the whole physiology and is enhanced by challenge and inhibited by threat.

Three instructional techniques are used with brain-based learning: *orchestrated immersion,* where a learning environment is created that immerses students in an educational experience; *relaxed alertness,* which attempts to eliminate fear in learners while at the same time maintaining a challenging environment; and *active processing,* which encourages learners to bring together and internalize information by actively processing it.[10]

Brain-based learning proponents would suggest that trainers use games that immerse participants in realistic, complex experiences, with meaningful challenge and immediate feedback, where they can safely practice new skills and behaviors. Sounds like a simulation-game to me.

Classic Learning Psychology (1,2,3)

Many classic principles of learning psychology are built into training with games. Factors like repetition, reinforcement, retention, and transference are all enhanced through the use of games. Games can provide for the repetition of new learning with practice, immediate feedback, and more practice, and also pair that repetition with positive reinforcement. Within the context of a game, key information can be restated, participants can practice a new model or a new approach several times with agreeable consequences, and positive associations and connections can be established. All of these will increase the probability that the new information, skills, and behaviors will be retained and applied back on the job.

The use of games can enhance and often expedite learning. "Among other things," write a variety of educators, "modern learning theory emphasizes the importance of immediate feedback, practice and review in the educational process. In a natural and enjoyable format, instructional games provide ample opportunity for all three."[11]

Constructivism (4,7,10)

Constructivism is an interesting learning philosophy established on the premise that, by reflecting on our experiences, we construct our own understanding of the world we live in.[12] Each of us produces our own rules and mental models, which are used to cohere our experiences. "Hence, learning is the process by which we adjust our mental models to accommodate new experiences. Constructivism sees learning as a search for meaning and suggests that learning start with a focusing on the issues around which students are actively trying to construct meaning."[13]

Under the theory of constructivism, trainers could use games to focus their learners on (1) making connections between facts and (2) developing new understanding. Trainers could tailor the debriefing process following a game to student responses and encourage students to analyze and interpret their learning. Trainers would also have to rely heavily on open-ended questions and promote extensive dialogue among students during a debriefing to be aligned with constructivism.

Similar to constructivism is transformative learning, which stresses the importance of experience, critical reflection, and rational discussion. Recent writings in the field describe how to help different learners integrate new learning with their existing knowledge, beliefs, and experiences. Certainly, experience, critical reflection, and rational discussion are central to experiential learning games and the debriefing of such games.

Control Theory (5,9)

This theory of motivation, championed by William Glasser, a well-known psychiatrist, contends that behavior is never caused by a response to an outside stimulus. Instead, control theory sees behavior as inspired by what a person wants most at any given time. These wants are triggered by five basic human needs: survival, love, power, fun, and freedom. According to Glasser, if students are not motivated to do their schoolwork, it's because they view schoolwork as irrelevant to their basic human needs. Teachers who follow control theory rely on cooperative, active learning techniques that enhance the power of the learners.[14]

It is interesting to note that when I first read about control theory, it was in a short article surveying current learning theories. The article listed only four of the basic human needs cited above. When I read Glasser's book, *The Quality School,* I was pleasantly surprised to see that he gives five basic human needs. The fifth human need that had somehow gotten left out of the article was the need for fun. Not every learning game can appeal to the learner's basic need for survival, love, power, and freedom, but we can certainly design and deliver learning games that appeal to the need for fun.[15]

Enhancement of Understanding (6,7,9)

In his work, *The Disciplined Mind,* Harvard professor Howard Gardner stresses the importance of understanding in learning and he presents four approaches to enhance learner understanding. The first, which he calls Learning from Suggestive Institutions, includes opportunities for hands-on experiences, which may reveal ways in which a learner's current thinking is inadequate. Direct Confrontations of Erroneous Conceptions is his second approach. This "challenge to a deeply held belief at least compels attention; and efforts to defend that belief, or to discover a better belief, line the most promising routes toward enhanced understanding."[16]

These two approaches to the enhancement of understanding bring to mind the second of Gredler's four general academic purposes for games that we considered in Chapter 1: to identify gaps or weaknesses in knowledge/skills. And certainly, a learning game that provides participants with hands-on, physical experiencing of gaps in their knowledge can be very powerful. For example, *Diversity Bingo,* an experiential learning game, has players searching for other players who will fit certain diversity categories.[17] As people play the game, they begin to realize things about themselves and the assumptions that they make regarding other people. Some players make even more startling discoveries about how other people see them and the assumptions that other people make about them. Such raising of awareness opens many players to a whole new level of understanding about diversity issues.

Gardner further suggests that with "spirited conversations, and proper guidance, a more appropriate theory can arise in the mind of the learner."[18] And, as we will discuss in Chapter 5, that is just what a skillful debriefing of a powerful game can bring about. The debriefing process following the game, *Diversity Bingo,* is filled with spirited conversations; and, with proper guidance, new ways of considering diversity issues can arise in the minds of the learners.

Gardner's third approach he calls A Framework that Facilitates Understanding in which he proposes that students ought to be exposed to examples of understanding and should be given ample opportunities to practice and perform their own understandings. This is reflected in Gredler's first academic purpose of a game: "to practice and/or refine knowledge/skills already acquired."[19]

Multiple Entry Points to Understanding, Gardner's fourth approach, takes advantage of the fact that "individuals possess different kinds of minds, featuring different blends of mental representations."[20] This is basically a call for a variety of learning techniques that appeal to all types of perceiving and understanding. Games often demand the use of different senses and different ways of perceiving. Such a call for a variety of learning approaches is given in many other theories as well.

Learning Styles (6,10)

This theory of learning also emphasizes the fact that individuals perceive and process information in very different ways. The ways of doing so are generally classified by learning styles theorists as concrete perceivers, abstract perceivers, active processors, and reflective processors. Traditional schools and traditional training techniques tend to favor abstract perceiving and reflective processing. This school of thought would advise teachers and trainers to design their instructional methods to connect with all four learning styles, using various combinations of experience, reflection, conceptualization, and experimentation. A well-designed game with a skillful debriefing can do just that.

Multiple Intelligences (6)

This theory of human intelligence, also developed by psychologist Howard Gardner, suggests that there are at least eight ways (at last count) that people have of perceiving and understanding the world. Gardner "labels each of these ways a distinct 'intelligence'—in other words, a set of skills allowing individuals to find and resolve genuine problems they face."[21]

"The eight intelligences are: Verbal-linguistic; logical-mathematical; visual-spatial; body-kinesthetic; musical-rhythmic; interpersonal; intrapersonal; and naturalist. Gardner advocates instructional methods

that appeal to all the intelligences, including role playing, musical performance, cooperative learning, reflection, visualization, story telling,
and so on."[22] Training games can certainly be designed to appeal to a
variety of Gardner's eight intelligences.

Neuroscience (6,9)

Neuroscience is the study of the human nervous system, the brain, and
the biological basis of consciousness, perception, memory, and learning. The nervous system and the brain are the physical foundation of
the human learning process. Neuroscience links our observations about
cognitive behavior with the actual physical processes that support such
behavior.

One of the key tenants of neuroscience is that the brain has a triadic
structure; "the Triune Brain" is a phrase coined by Dr. Paul MacLean
in 1973.[23] Neuroscience proposes that our brain actually contains three
brains: the lower or reptilian brain that controls basic sensory motor
functions; the mammalian or limbic brain that controls emotions,
memory, and biorhythms; and the neocortex or thinking brain that controls cognition, reasoning, language, and higher intelligence.

If educators were to take neuroscience into account, they would
organize a curriculum around real experiences and integrated, "whole"
ideas. Plus, they would focus on instruction that promotes complex
thinking and the "growth" of the brain. Neuroscientists advocate continued learning and intellectual development throughout adulthood.
They would probably be supportive of realistic, in-depth, complex,
experiential simulation games. Don't you think?

Right-Brain, Left-Brain, Whole Brain (6)

Right-brain, left-brain theories of the structure and functions of the
mind suggest that the two different sides of the brain control two different "modes" of thinking. They also suggest that each of us prefers
one mode to the other. To foster a more whole-brained learning experience, teachers and trainers would use instruction techniques that connect with both sides of the brain. They could increase their classroom's
right-brain learning activities by incorporating more patterning,
metaphors, analogies, role-playing, visuals, and movement into their
reading, calculation, and analytical activities.[24]

Ned Hermann and his whole brain theory suggest a four-quadrant model of the brain that includes the A-quadrant analyzer, the B-quadrant organizer, the C-quadrant personalizer, and the D-quadrant visualizer. Hermann proposes a whole brain approach to the design and delivery of learning.[25] Such learning in the form of training games would include material and approaches that were analytical and logical, organized and detailed, interpersonal and intuitive, and imaginative and big-picture, thus covering all four quadrants.

Small-Group Dynamics (7,8,10)

Small-group dynamics is an area of educational psychology particularly pertinent to training games. Being able to manage groups effectively is a key skill for all trainers and is certainly important to the effective use of games. Much of the writing and research on small-group dynamics has been the foundation for the established techniques of managing training games. These include guidelines like establishing ground rules, creating a climate for learning, keeping activities on track, ensuring full participation, and debriefing activities.[26]

Learning in groups has been a subject of interest in adult education for a long time, but recent research and writing in adult education has looked at "groups as learning environments" and at group learning as opposed to individual learning. Collaborative learning, cooperative learning, and action learning theories have all moved from the theoretical to the practical in numerous organizations and corporate training programs as well.

Collaborative learning refers to small-group instruction in which there is interdependence among students, promotion of each member's learning, individual accountability, and use of "small-group" techniques to foster social skills and learning. Cooperative learning approaches are usually less individually focused, emphasize working together, and often have group accountability. Action learning seems to take much of its theoretical basis from both transformative and collaborative learning and is being used in organizational training and development efforts in the United States and abroad. Action Learning has received a lot of attention in the United Kingdom in particular.

In action learning, reflection is seen as the precursor to effective action and there is a very deliberate attempt to reflect and learn from experience, and then apply what has been learned by taking action. "Action learning is a continuous process of learning and reflection, supported by colleagues, with an intention of getting things done. Through action learning, individuals learn with and from each other by working on real problems and reflecting on their own experiences. The process helps us to take an active stance towards life and helps to overcome the tendency to think, feel and be passive towards the pressures of life."[27]

Action learning involves a group of people (called a set) working together for a concentrated period of time. The people in the set work with one another to better understand their work situations, and to explore and analyze the problems, issues, and various pressures they face.[28] There are surely parallels between certain aspects of action learning and collaborative learning and the phenomenon of work teams and project teams in the workplace today. The whole concept of "team building" and developing "team skills" reflects many of the attributes of collaborative learning. Team training has been one of the highest growth areas for training games. This combination of adult and group psychology, team training, and training games should continue in importance for some time to come.

Beyond team training and team building, many aspects of action learning and collaborative approaches are found in experiential training activities. The particular importance of a deliberating and thorough debriefing and the reflecting of the learning group on the experience they have just undergone are supported by these theories and approaches. It is also interesting to note, in an article by Shari Caudron entitled, "Learners Speak Out" in *Training and Development* magazine, that after surveying many of the current adult learning theories as well as collecting anecdotal information from successful professionals, the point is made that adults learn best by having experiences and reflecting on them.[29] Experiential games and simulation games with thoughtful, in-depth debriefing would be well supported here.

Social Learning Theory (1,8)

Social learning theory, also called observational learning, occurs when an observer's behavior changes after viewing the behavior of a model. Learning by observation involves four separate processes: attention, retention, production, and motivation. For learning to occur or be enhanced, learners must get a chance to observe and model behaviors that lead to positive reinforcement. Educators need to encourage collaborative learning, since much of learning happens within important social and environmental contexts.[30]

As you can easily see, there is much repetition and overlapping among learning theories; and many of the learning theories give support to the use of training games. The design and delivery of effective training should ideally be based on a variety of learning theories and stimulate as many modalities and senses as possible. Games are ideal learning tools to do just that. Figure 2.1 is a matrix illustrating the various learning theories and the learning criteria they support.

Final Thoughts

There's more to playing a training game than winning and losing. There's even more than pleasure in the playing. There is real learning that can take place. With a well-designed and well-delivered training game you can repeat and reinforce key learning concepts, provide safe practice of new skills, and let learners analyze, interpret, discuss, and reflect on new information—all in a challenging, stimulating, enjoyable context.

And speaking of challenging, stimulating, enjoyable contexts, wait until you see the wide range of training games available in the marketplace today. Chapter 3 will guide you through that territory and Chapter 4 will introduce you to the new regions of electronic training games. Then, in Chapter 5 as we take a look at choosing and using training games, we will include the learning theory criteria that we have discussed in this chapter in the selection and evaluation of training games.

Learning Theory Matrix

According to the learning theories listed on the right, for a training game to be effective, it should contain the characteristics listed below. The characteristics have received check marks under the learning theories that support them. An effective training game should:

Characteristic	ACCELERATED LEARNING	ADULT LEARNING THEORY	BRAIN-BASED LEARNING	CLASSIC LEARNING THEORY	CONSTRUCTIVISM	CONTROL THEORY	ENHANCE UNDERSTANDING	LEARNING STYLES	MULTIPLE INTELLIGENCES	NEUROSCIENCE	RIGHT-LEFT-WHOLE BRAIN	SMALL-GROUP DYNAMICS	SOCIAL LEARNING THEORY
1. Repeat and reinforce key information			✓	✓									
2. Give immediate feedback			✓	✓									
3. Provide safe practice of new skills			✓	✓									
4. Develop understanding of new concepts			✓		✓								
5. Provide meaningful challenge	✓	✓				✓							
6. Stimulate as many senses as possible							✓	✓	✓		✓		
7. Promote extensive dialogue and discussion		✓			✓		✓						
8. Furnish social contact and group work		✓	✓									✓	✓
9. Immerse in realistic, complex experiences							✓			✓			
10. Provide analysis, interpretation, reflection					✓		✓	✓					

FIGURE 2.1

In a Nutshell

Everyone likes to win. But there's more to a good game than winning. There is *pleasure in the playing*. Along with the pleasure in the playing, there are other unique benefits that games can bring to your training program. Games are fun and dynamic; they provide a safe arena for practice. Games make the learning concrete and give time to let the learning sink in. They encourage socializing, level the playing field, and make training more appealing. They also allow the trainer a "time out," while letting the trainer monitor the learning.

Designing training games that include any of the characteristics listed below, which are supported by numerous learning theories, will reinforce the learning taking place in those games:

1. Repeat and reinforce key information

2. Give immediate feedback

3. Provide safe practice of new skills

4. Develop understanding of new concepts

5. Provide meaningful challenge

6. Stimulate as many senses as possible

7. Promote extensive dialogue and discussion

8. Furnish social contact and group work

9. Provide realistic, complex experiences

10. Include analysis, interpretation, reflection

Notes

1. Ken Jones, *Interactive Learning Events: A Guide for Facilitators* (London: Kogan Page, 1988). (Distributed in the United States by Stylus Publishing.)

2. Marc Prensky, *Digital Game-Based Learning* (New York: McGraw-Hill, 2001).

3. Ibid.

4. Margaret Parkin, *Tales for Trainers* (London: Kogan Page, 1998). (Distributed in the United States by Stylus Publishing.)

5. David Meier, "Accelerated Learning," in *Executive Directions Newsletter* (New York: Executive Directions, Inc. 1994.)

6. Susan Imel, "New Views of Adult Learning," in *Trends and Issues Alert* (ERIC Clearinghouse of Adult, Career and Vocational Education, 1999).

7. Malcolm Knowles, *The Adult Learner,* 5th ed. (Houston, TX: Gulf Publishing Company, 1998).

8. Steven Leib, "Adults as Learners," *Principles of Adult Learning,* www.hcc.hawaii.edu, 2000.

9. Ruth Palombo Weiss, "Brain-Based Learning," *Training and Development Journal* 54, no. 7 (2000):21–24.

10. On Purpose Associates, "About Learning/Theories," *How Do People Learn?* www.Funderstanding.com, 1998.

11. John Greer, Irise Schwartzberg, and Virginia Laycock, *Motivating Learners with Instructional Games,* Dubuque, IA: Kendall/Hunt Publishing, 1977).

12. Sharan B. Merriam, and Rosemary S. Caffarella, *Learning in Adulthood* (San Francisco, CA: Jossey-Bass Publishers, 1999).

13. On Purpose Associates, "About Learning/Theories."

14. William Glasser, *The Quality School* (New York: Harper and Row, 1990).

15. Ibid.

16. Howard Gardner, *The Disciplined Mind: What All Students Should Understand* (New York: Simon & Schuster, 1999).

17. Susan El-Shamy and Gayle Stuebe, *Diversity Bingo* (Bloomington, IN: Advancement Strategies, Inc., and San Francisco, CA: Pfieffer/Jossey-Bass, 1990).

18. Howard Gardner, *The Disciplined Mind.*

19. Margaret Gredler, *Designing and Evaluating Games and Simulations,* (Houston, TX: Gulf Publishing, 1994).

20. Howard Gardner, *The Disciplined Mind.*

21. On Purpose Associates, "About Learning/Theories."

22. Ibid.

23. John Giles, "Learning How We Learn," *Gower Handbook of Training and Development,* edited by John Prior (London: Gower Publishing, 1999).

24. On Purpose Associates, "About Learning/Theories."

25. Ned Hermann, *The Whole Brain Business Book* (New York: McGraw-Hill, 1996).

26. Joe E. Heimlich, "Constructing Group Learning," *Learning in Groups: Exploring Fundamental Principles, New Uses and Emerging Opportunities,* no. 71, edited by Susan Imel (San Francisco, CA: Jossey-Bass Publishers, 1996).

27. Ian McGill, and Liz Beaty, *Action Learning,* (London: Kogan Page, 1995). (Distributed in the United States by Stylus Publishing.)

28. Ibid.

29. Shari Caudron, "Learners Speak Out," *Training and Development Journal* 54, no. 4 (2000):52–57.

30. On Purpose Associates, "About Learning Theories."

If you were to go game hunting through the stacks of games and puzzles in our family collection, you might overlook our Scrabble game. The textured, dark red box is dented, cracked, and turning black from wear along the edges. The corners of the box are held together by tape over tape and the inside has yellowed with age. There are remnants of masking tape around the middle of the box from its four journeys across the ocean. But the letters and the racks are made of wood and the game board still works. The Scrabble game always sits on top of the stack of games, maybe because it's the smallest box and that's the natural order of things, or maybe because it's played the most and has earned its position as "top game" and that's the natural order of things.

3

BIG GAME HUNTING

TYPES OF TRAINING GAMES

For anyone beginning the journey into the land of training games, that first encounter can boggle the mind. Some of you may remember the good "ole" days when *Games Trainers Play* was not only the best title ever for a book of training games, but also the only affordable resource for training games. Or, if you worked for a large corporation, the training department may have invested in yearly annuals of human resources development tools that included a number of learning activities, many of which were games.

Today, the sheer number of interactive training games and activities available in the training and development marketplace is astounding. A quick survey of the bookshelves devoted to "business management" at any major national bookstore will produce ten to twenty volumes of training games. And for some reason, a majority of these are oversized, which if nothing else, makes them easy to find, since they have to be kept on the top shelves.

A few minutes online with Amazon.com will produce another plethora of "training games," although these can be difficult to find at first until you learn to use the phrases "management games," "business games," and "interactive corporate training games" in your search. If you go to a training-specific Web site such as TrainSeek.com, some training games are found under games/simulations in the training tools category and others are listed as books or training materials under various training topics. And, if you are on the mailing lists of the training and development catalog publishers, you have no doubt found yourself thumbing through the various sections entitled "training games," "team-building games," and "training resources."

And, as if all of the above is not difficult enough, you will immediately notice that not everything called a game is a game and many of the products that have the word "game" in their title have few, if any, games among their offerings. Learning games are often combined with learning activities and simulations, as in *101 Games and Activities*. While this may not make a difference (after all, what you want is an effective, interactive learning event), it does add to the difficulty of surveying and classifying training games!

As I noted earlier, many of the games in the original 1980 edition of *Games Trainers Play* are not games, in the sense that we have defined games. In fact, in their introduction, Newstrom and Scannell wrote, "In this book, a game may be an exercise, illustration, activity, or incident used to present or support the trainee's learning."[1]

Since the greatest number of interactive learning compendiums are those that combine games and activities, my own included, let me say a few words here about learning activities. Learning activities are great and they have many of the same effective qualities as games. They can involve the learner, present ideas and content effectively, and reinforce learning. A good activity, like a good game, will have a purpose, a procedure, rules or guidelines. They should be followed by a debriefing session. But learning activities are basically games without the competitive element. There is no scoring mechanism that leads to winning and losing. And, to a fair degree, the "fantasy world" element will be missing as well.

In a learning activity, instead of accumulating so many points in a set time period and being the first person or group to do so, people or groups are asked to complete an activity. When you are done, you are done. You don't win or lose an activity. Throughout a training session, too many activities, like too many games, can become wearisome, and just how many of each to include in your training program is a design issue.

However, it should be mentioned here that many learning activities could easily be changed into games by adding additional structure, competition, a system of measurement, enforced time limits, and prizes. This is something you may want to consider when you have a good activity but feel the need for a more vigorous, involving exercise. For the purposes of this book, we are looking at training games: learning activities in which players compete, according to rules within a given context, and win by accomplishing a measurable goal using skills and competencies that are applicable beyond the game itself to the particular course content.

Attempting to categorize the abundance and variety of games in some way that would be helpful to a person new to exploring the field is a little overwhelming at first. One approach that has been taken by some in the field is to categorize training games according to the paraphernalia or materials used to play the games, such as paper-and-pencil games, board games, card games, computer games, and so on. Another approach is to classify them by what actually happens or what people do in the games, for example, experiential games, discussion games, role-playing games, simulation games, and so on. An additional system that you will notice when you look through catalogs and browse through bookshelves, virtual or otherwise, is categorizing by subject matter, such as team-building games, leadership games, management games, or categorizing by use within training programs, for instance, warm-up and ice-breaker games, opening and closing games, and introductory games.

One further aspect to be considered in our journey is "interactivity." There are training games that can be played by individuals alone, but, for our purposes, we will be looking primarily at training games that are played by groups of people, where the interactivity is among individuals or groups and not between an individual and a machine. In the realm of computer games and multimedia learning, interactivity has come to mean the individual's interacting with the material via the electronic machine. Chapter 4 will look at electronic training games, where the interactivity is among individuals and machines, but right now, let's look at the vast array of nonelectronic training games.

For our purposes, I have divided training games into four categories that I hope will be helpful. This division is determined by two factors: (1) how the learning occurs and (2) what is required of the trainer. By "how the learning occurs," I mean, does the learning occur primarily through the interaction of the learner with content material or does the learning take place through the actual physical experience of the learner? By "what is required of the trainer," I mean, does the trainer purchase or design the game and then facilitate the game, or, does the trainer purchase the game frame or template, insert content into that frame or template, and then facilitate it?

If we put these two factors into a matrix, it would appear as shown in Figure 3.1.

As we look at these four categories of training games, I will offer examples and illustrations. All of the example games presented in this chapter are listed and further described in the first section of Chapter 8, "Games Galore."

Let's start with content-focused games. In general, and in terms of what is required of the trainer, content-focused games are often the easiest games to purchase and to use. They require no design time, and trainers at all experience levels can use them effectively. And, with the large number of such games available on the marketplace, you can choose a game that you feel comfortable with from a very wide selection.

1. Content-Focused Games

In content-focused games, the subject content of the game is the focal point; the game has been designed specifically to enhance and expedite

Training Games Matrix		
Learning occurs through:	Trainer is required to:	
	Facilitate given content	Insert content and facilitate
the learner's interaction with the content	1. Content-Focused Games	3. Content-Focused Frame Games
the learner's physical experiencing of the content	2. Experiential Games	4. Experiential Frame Games

FIGURE 3.1

the learning of that particular content. Participants or players of the game follow given rules in a given context and employ the paraphernalia used by that game to move toward achieving a set goal that determines winning. The trainer's role is to facilitate the game, that is, to introduce and explain it, to set it up and get it started, to manage or facilitate its being carried out, and to debrief what happened after the game is over. Throughout the debriefing, the learning that has occurred can be pointed out and, thus, further reinforced. Although there is always some learning that occurs through the act of playing, the major learning comes from focusing on and interacting with the subject matter.

There are numerous types of content-focused games. Many of these are better known by the paraphernalia used in playing them, such as paper-and-pencil games, matrix games, television quiz show games, board games, and card games. You will also find much overlapping within these categories. However, let's investigate some of these different types of content-focused games and consider the appropriate or effective uses they have.

Paper-and-Pencil Games

As the name implies, paper-and-pencil games use paper and pencils. Most of the paper-and-pencil techniques used in training are activities, but a few are games and many can be turned into games. Such games and activities usually present quizzes, puzzles, or some type of information printed on paper that individuals or groups must complete, solve, or manipulate in some way within a given time frame and according to a set of rules. Learning occurs either by the printed material on the paper reflecting the content of the training or by the activity itself requiring the use of a skill being developed in the training. The trainer introduces the game, manages the game, and debriefs the game when it is over.

Early in a training program, paper-and-pencil quizzes can be a non-threatening way to identify gaps or weaknesses in knowledge or skills. For example, a true-or-false quiz covering a variety of concepts and misconceptions on the topic being taught could be a fun way to identify what participants do and do not know on the topic. The participants can be divided into three or four small groups, and each group receives a copy of the quiz for the group members to work on during a set time period. When time is up, the groups can grade their own papers as the instructor goes over the correct answers. The group with the most right answers wins a prize. It's quick; it's fun; it's easy. Participants get a quick idea of what they know and don't know, and so do you.

Short paper-and-pencil puzzles can be used effectively to illustrate a concept or a behavior pattern or to bring forth habits that inhibit or obstruct learning. For example, at one time or another most of you have probably been in a training situation where you were presented with a geometric illustration and asked to "find the 35 triangles" or the "40 squares." This type of activity can be used to bring forth habits that inhibit or obstruct learning and, thus, illustrate our tendency to jump to early conclusions and the difficulty most of us have in perceiving something from many points of view. Such an activity can be turned into a game by providing some type of a story line, by giving ten minutes to accomplish the task, and by offering a small prize to any person or group that finds the given number of triangles or squares.

"Hidden Squares" in Newstrom and Scannell's *Games Trainers Play* is an example of this type of paper-and-pencil game.[2] Participants are shown or given a drawing of a large square divided into smaller squares and asked to count the number of squares that they see. Participants usually report varying numbers of squares depending on whether they count only the squares that are immediately evident or "dig deeper" into the problem and count squares that are made up of groups of squares within the drawing.

Paper-and-pencil games can be employed to practice using knowledge and skills being acquired in the training. Groups or individuals can be given a list of information that needs to be transformed in some way. The transformation might require the application of certain rules that are being studied, or the use of a model that is being considered. Individuals can be given a certain amount of time to generate answers on the list itself or small groups might put their answers on posted flip chart paper. When the time is up, the instructor can help the whole group generate the right answers and grade their own work. Individuals or groups who have all the right answers can take their own prizes from a bowl of sweets.

Paper-and-pencil games can also be used as a quick and easy review technique. For example, at the end of a training session you can allow small groups of participants ten minutes to complete a fill-in-the-blank test that covers key class material. Afterwards you can go through the test with the group discussing the answers and giving prizes to groups for every right answer they have. Give a "grand prize" to the group with the most right answers. (Be sure the prizes are items that can be easily shared by a few people!) It never ceases to amaze me how motivated people can become to win prizes, and this simple technique leaves participants energized and positive at the end of a class, rather than lulled and dulled by a liturgy of "key learnings."

Matrix games are a type of paper-and-pencil game that requires participants to cover boxes on a matrix by demonstrating a specific skill or knowledge. The most recognizable form of matrix is the Bingo format of twenty-five boxes formed by five rows and five columns. Boxes can be considered "covered" by various means: filling in an answer, demonstrating a behavior, and having a judge or fellow player sign the box. As participants get five right answers in a row, or column, or diagonally across their cards, they receive a prize.

Graham Roberts-Phelps, in his *Health and Safety Games,* uses a simple nine-box matrix in a game he calls "Safety Bingo Quiz" where participants first choose nine numbers between one and twenty-five and place them anywhere in the grid.[3] The instructor then reads questions numbered one through twenty-five and when participants hear a question with one of their numbers, they write down the answer to that question in the appropriate square. This is such a simple design, but it is so effective. It can be used as an icebreaker to get things started in a fun way, as an "assessment" tool to ascertain knowledge gaps early in training, or as a summary activity at the end of a program.

Paper-and-pencil games have many advantages. They are quick and easy, flexible and adaptable, and inexpensive. They can be used with almost any subject matter and in a wide range of situations. They also work well with individuals, small groups, and very large groups. Sometimes, I begin a paper-and-pencil activity or game by having participants work individually, and then, after a few minutes, suggest they get a partner: "Two heads are better than one." Finally, I might ask every set of partners to combine with another set of partners and share answers and work as a group for the last three minutes. The first group finished and/or the group with the most right answers gets a grand prize. Other groups that finish within the time limit and/or get almost all the right answers get a smaller prize.

The disadvantage of paper-and-pencil games is a tendency to seem childish or to remind participants of elementary school activities, especially if the printed materials are not well done or look amateurish. There is also an inclination not to hold a debriefing session after paper-and-pencil games; and therefore, no overt link is made to the class learning objectives. This can lead to participants seeing the game as "just fun and games" and not recognizing the learning value it contains.

Card Games

Card games are competitive activities that use specially constructed decks of cards, sometimes called "learning cards" or "discussion cards." The games focus on the content of these cards, which contain subject matter from the training. Some card games involve manipulating the cards in some way, such as sorting or rank ordering them. Other card games involve the accomplishing of a task or the answering of general questions related to the content of the cards. The trainer's role in most card games is to facilitate the game by introducing it, watching over it, and debriefing when the game is over. The major learning in most card games comes from interacting with card content.

One of the most appealing qualities of learning cards is that they are tactile. The interaction between the learners and the cards is involving. The learner's being able to manipulate the cards—to shuffle, handle, arrange, rearrange, and literally play with the cards—adds a tremendous personal absorption to the process and can thus enhance the learning. By combining this tactile quality with gaming instructions to order, or rank, or sort, or respond to the cards in some way, a variety of very intense games and activities can be devised.

This tactile quality is present to some extent in board games that use decks of cards and tokens. Some card games are rather like board games without the board. That is, the cards are used as a means of practicing and refining participant knowledge of concepts and principles; but instead of moving a pawn around a game board, participants draw cards and follow the rules they have been given regarding the use of the card content.

There are endless possibilities for card content. Cards can present the characteristics of something. For example, they can give the characteristics of an effective leader or an effective team. Cards can give facts or data about the subject matter. They can present situations for discussion or problem solving, strategies or techniques for accomplishing a task, or multiple-choice questions for discussion and answering. There are also many possibilities for card game tasks. Such tasks can involve assessing yourself or your work environment, carrying out some type of artistic performance, and/or implementing the card content in some way back in the workplace.

As an example, in a coaching class I teach, I use decks of *Performance Improvement Cards.*[4] Each deck contains fifty-two different examples of workplace situations reflecting a need for performance improvement. I like to "stack the deck," so I usually go through the decks ahead of time and pull out twenty to twenty-five situation cards that I feel are most relevant to the group. I then set these decks of cards aside until it's time to use them for the game.

For the game that I call "Friendly Feedback" and that is really a variation on a feedback practice activity in *An Instructor's Guide to Action Packs,*[5] I give each small group a full deck of cards or one of my "stacked decks." I have them shuffle their decks; then, one at a time group members draw a card and read it aloud. Each person has two minutes after drawing a card to verbally use the coaching model being taught in that class as if they are at a coaching session with the person on the card. If they accomplish this in two minutes or less, they get five points. If it takes more than two minutes, but they do accomplish it, they get three points. If they can't do it on their own, group members can help them and they get two points.

The groups do their own scoring and have fifty minutes to draw cards and practice the model. When the time is up, any group with thirty or more points gets a prize and the group with the most points gets a bonus prize. In fifty minutes, every person in the group has used the model or heard someone else use the model at least a dozen times in a variety of situations. In addition, they have had fun and won prizes!

One of the most unique uses of learning cards that I have seen in a long time is the *Design Patterns Playing Cards*,[6] a card deck designed by Joshua Kerievsky, the founder of Industrial Logic, that is used to teach and reinforce player skills at designing software using the art of combining patterns. Kerievsky's game, "Patterns Poker," is an innovative combination of poker, storytelling, and learning. (For more information, see the annotated games list in Chapter 8.) This fun game has players making use of this exceptional card deck to reinforce concepts and to hone their design skills. Pretty clever, ehh?

The advantages of card games include the high involvement of using cards; the flexibility the trainer has in using only certain cards that seem most appropriate or needed; and the variety of games and activities that can be devised around a particular set of cards. On the other hand, some card content can become outdated quickly; and new cards or decks may need to be prepared periodically. And, although card games and activities can work well with groups of all sizes, the larger the group, the more structured the game needs to be, the larger the sheer number of cards necessary becomes, and the greater the chances are of lost and damaged cards.

There are a variety of card decks and card games available in the marketplace. Most of these are on general topics such as team development, leadership, creativity, and customer service. These decks can be shuffled, stacked, sorted, and resorted. They can be used time and time again, or they are sometimes used in class and then given to participants as take-away items for use beyond the class. Trainers can also make their own decks of cards. Using construction paper put through your printer and cut into cards can work very well and allows you to have very specific content. Making your own cards also works well if you have content that needs to be modified for each group you are training. (For more exact instructions on creating your own card games, see Chapter 7.)

Board Games

Perhaps more than any other type of training game format, the board game carries the most positive associations. We have all played board games in our childhood, and many of us still enjoy hours of engaging entertainment with board games for adults. For this reason, people may accept the playing of a learning board game more easily. Ken Jones' description of "the 'closed environment,' of an unreal world which completely justifies the behaviour . . ."[7] seems to apply to training board games as well as board games that are strictly entertainment.

"Board games are a unique experience. They not only present a learning experience but are a different world unto themselves," explains Steve Sugar, president of the Game Group. "What the players experience—a heightened interaction with the material and other players—was more than just a different approach to learning. For a short period of time the players were transported into an entirely different learning environment.[8]

In the *Oxford History of Board Games*, David Parlett distinguishes between two types of board games: "positional games such as *Chess, Draughts,* and *Backgammon,* where the play of the game centres entirely on the relative positions of pieces on the board itself," and "theme games such as *Monopoly, Cluedo,* and *Diplomacy,*" where their defining feature is that they are "representational and may involve elements of role-play and quasi-dramatic performance." Parlett continues, "Typically, the board and pieces account for only part of the equipment, and often for only a small part at that, and the play of the game centres, so to speak, 'above' the board, in the minds and interactions of the players themselves."[9]

Many training board games are what Parlett defines as "theme games," and often based on popular formats used by many recreational games. Participants sit around a flat game board, roll dice, move tokens around the board, draw cards, and answer questions. The content of the cards may be subject matter oriented, as may be the content on the board itself or the "spaces" on the board. There may or may not be an overt theme, but certainly a theme enhances the "world unto itself" feeling.

Board games are an excellent means of practicing and refining participant knowledge of concepts and principles. They also work very well for practicing the application of models that have been covered in the training. One of the first board games I ever designed came from the need to have participants in a supervisory skills class practice an effective feedback model. By using a simple game board that had a square with the word "Start," followed by another twenty-five squares going around the board and coming back to a final square with the word "Finish" on it, dice and a deck of situation cards, class members practiced using the feedback model over and over and had fun doing so. After using the game board a time or two, I learned the fun value of enhancing a few squares with messages like "You called the employee an idiot! Go back 5 squares!" and "You have been named Supervisor of the Year! Go ahead 4 squares!"

The Lead Group International has a wonderful set of board games designed around a three-dimensional performance model covering head (analytical and technical expertise), heart (positive relationships), and courage (embracing change, taking risks, and taking action). The game boards are artistic, clever, and involving and the card decks used in the games present case studies that require participants to solve problems and make decisions. These board games feature journey themes with titles like *The Customer Journey, The Sales Journey,* and *The Leadership Journey.*[10] The Lead Group International has done an excellent job of designing and integrating complete learning experiences that center on the use of these wonderful game boards.

Game boards have other advantages besides being very involving for the players. They are relatively easy to design, quite portable, and do not take up excessive space in the training environment. While not as flexible as card games, they can be designed for more than one type of game and can also be modified in terms of the length of time needed for playing. For a board game to be involving and motivating, there must be some challenge to it. It cannot be too easily won. Providing the right blend of skill, knowledge, and chance can be very important and not always easy. Since most board games are designed for use by two to six players, when they are used with larger groups, many copies of the game board and the various required equipment will be needed. That can be expensive and/or time consuming, but not prohibitively so.

Other Content-Focused Games

The following are a few more categories of content-focused games. There are others, as well as combinations of the various categories.

Acting Games   Acting games are games that involve acting out specific behaviors, usually behaviors being developed in the class. Such games include role-playing activities that have points awarded for using certain behaviors and for meeting set criteria within certain time limits. Improvisational and enactment games have participants using certain behaviors and/or applying certain models within specified settings, for example, "pretend you are in a department meeting," or "you will be acting out a debate." Acting games are similar to simulations but they involve competition, and they do not have participants acting as themselves in an ongoing role, but acting out a particular behavior in a short period of time to acquire points or meet some criteria to win.

In "Meeting Simulation," one of the games in *Card Games for Developing Teams* that Advancement Strategies published with Gower Publications,[11] participants take assigned agenda items and act out a meeting. They have a set time to persuade the group of the importance of their agenda item. Of course to do so, they must really understand their item; and the other participants have to listen carefully and try to understand in order to vote on the most important. It is incredible how involved participants can become when they are "only pretending." They can exaggerate and vent some of their frustrations about meetings and still play the game and learn about the content!

Acting games are flexible, adaptable, easy to prepare, and quite inexpensive. In addition, they provide an energizing departure from standard training delivery models. On the downside, they can be intimidating to the more quiet and retiring of participants and can provide a stage for the louder, more attention-seeking participants. A structured approach with exacting rules or guidelines can help.

Artistic Games Artistic games are games that use some form of art-work, such as drawing, painting, sketching, collage making, and so on. These competitive activities require participants to meet some type of challenge within guidelines and time frames to produce artwork related in some way to course content. For example, games and contests can require participants to produce posters or wall charts reflecting examples of principles or techniques from the course content. Or, as a summary exercise, small groups might be given guidelines, time constraints, and limited materials in which to produce a work of art that illustrates key concepts from the program content.

One of my favorite artistic games is the "Full-Page Ad" game in *Card Games for Developing Service.*[12] This game is an excellent summary activity for programs on customer service. It uses the Service Interaction Cards, which contain twenty-six cards giving things to do for better service interactions and twenty-six cards giving things not to do. The group is divided into smaller groups of three to four participants each. After shuffling the "do" cards, I deal a few cards to each group and give them large sheets of flip chart paper and multicolored marker pens. They then have twenty minutes to choose one behavior from their cards and draw a "full-page ad" promoting that particular customer service behavior. When "showtime" is announced, the groups tape their ads to the wall and, one-by-one, present them to the whole group. The ads can be incredibly clever and make a very memorable summary. A great variation of this activity is to have the group create a collage advertisement using colored paper, sticks and strings, buttons, paper clips, stickers of all sorts, and whatever else I throw in at the last minute.

Artistic games are flexible, adaptable, and easy to prepare; they require no additional space and few materials. The products of artistic games and activities can decorate the walls of the classroom and be used at the end of a training session to help summarize the learning. Even though many participants may see themselves as "non-artistic," when such games and activities are done in small groups, everyone can participate in some way. A drawback to artistic games is participant reluctance to appear incompetent, but this can usually be dealt with fairly easily.

Wall Games and Flip Chart Games Wall games and flip chart games are games that use posters mounted on the wall, or pages from flip charts, as the focus of the game. These posters might literally be a vertical version of a game board or a matrix card or they might be elaborate illustrations that require players to find hidden meanings or messages within the poster. Some wall games require players to write or draw on the poster; others are large puzzle games or mazes.

Graham Roberts-Phelps, in his *Health and Safety Games for Trainers,*[13] has a game called "Caption Competition" that I like to use with posters rather than handouts. Participants compete in this game to come up with the funniest captions for pictures related to health and safety issues at work. I like to take such pictures, cartoons, or humorous drawings and enlarge them onto poster-sized paper for ongoing competitions during workshops and programs. Participants can use sticky notes to write captions and post them under the drawings throughout the day. At the end of the day, some type of voting can be used to choose the winners for each poster.

Wall games and flip chart games are simple, easy to use, and inexpensive. They provide a nice variety to more standard activities and appeal to the more visual learners. Drawbacks of wall games and flip chart games are those associated with the type of game illustrated on them. Also, some participants in large groups may have difficulty seeing if only one chart is used. Many of the games, however, can make use of multiple charts positioned around the room.

Construction Games Construction games are games that require the players to build a three-dimensional object of some sort. Various materials are used in construction games. Interlocking building toys are quite popular construction material, as are modeling clay, construction paper, tongue depressors, pipe cleaners, and old newspapers, to name just a few. Construction games can be used for summation or review purposes with the object being created being something that represents a concept or ideal from the training. Or the major construction activity itself might require the practice of skills and behaviors being taught in the program. Construction games can also be used to raise awareness of weaknesses in knowledge or skills.

In a game called "Build a Paper Plane," in his book *Training Games—from the Inside*,[14] Jeff Stibbard asks individual participants or small groups of participants to make a paper plane fly across the room and hit a target. The activity can be used to illustrate the importance of testing and piloting, and, if groups are used, the importance of effective brainstorming. It can also be used to practice planning and/or brainstorming skills. Stibbard gives variations of the activity that make it more game-like, such as giving time limits, adding extra challenge by not allowing talking, and awarding prizes for hitting the target within the time limit.

Construction games can add variety to training programs. There are always participants whose kinesthetic learning styles respond well to such hands-on activities. The only caveat to keep in mind is not to overdo your creative use of various construction materials and end up with piles of messy materials strewn around the training room for the rest of the day.

Quiz Show Games   Quiz show games are games that mimic well-known television quiz shows and are used primarily to demonstrate or practice specific skills or knowledge. Currently the most popular formats for training quiz show games include *Jeopardy, Family Feud, Tic Tac Toe* and *Who Wants to be a Millionaire?* For example, using a *Who Wants to Be a Millionaire* format, you could divide a training class into teams and, as part of the review process, have each team devise questions of increasing difficulty based on the program content. Then the questions could be pooled for use in the contest and each team could choose a representative to compete. The game could be played in true "millionaire" style with prizes or fake money awarded at the end.

Quiz show games can be great fun and participants will often become highly involved. Although they can sometimes take a great deal of initial design time on the part of the trainer, once they are designed, it is not too difficult to update or replace their content. It is also important to periodically reflect on the amount of time spent in these types of games versus the actual learning that is taking place.

2. Experiential Games

Although we are looking specifically at games here, much of what is true for games is also true for any type of experiential activity. The major learning that occurs in experiential games and activities takes place through the actual physical experiencing of the learner. Learning occurs by doing, by feeling, and by experiencing. The focus of the learning is on the activity being carried out, not on specific content. The role of the trainer can be crucial to the overall learning experience of participants in an experiential game. Not only must the trainer introduce, set up, and manage the game, but the trainer must also pay close attention to the various dynamics that occur during the "playing of the game" in order to lead an insightful and discerning debriefing.

The role of the participants in an experiential game or activity is to experience. They physically move, do, and interact; and, in so doing, they experience the actual phenomenon that is being studied. The major learning comes from the experiencing of the phenomenon being studied and the debriefing of participant experiences. In the debriefing of a content-focused game, there is also learning that occurs from the experience of playing the game as well as the interaction with the content of the game; but it is not the major learning, it is a learning by-product of interaction. However, in an experiential game, it is the other way around. The major learning is from the experience, and content can furnish additional learning. There are also games that provide big doses of both types of learning—experiential games that also have large amounts of content-focused material, such as elaborate or in-depth simulation games.

Since experiential games include experiencing the phenomenon being studied and involve the feelings and reactions of participants to events within the game, they can be more difficult to utilize and require a sensitive, skillful debriefing process. They can, however, be very powerful learning tools and a great enhancement to training programs. Most experiential games, when purchased, include extensive instructions for playing and debriefing the game. If you are a trainer who is new to the use of experiential games, I would suggest you cofacilitate

the experiential game you will be using at least a time or two before
you do it on your own.

Experiential games can range from short, simple, ten- or fifteen-
minute activities that provide enough experience for an hour debriefing,
all the way to day-long, complicated simulations requiring hours of
debriefing. And, of course, there is everything imaginable in between.
Again, it is difficult to categorize such games, but for illustrative purposes, let's try three categories: physical games, short activity games,
and simulation games. Let me state at this point that simulation games
are games that simulate particular real-life circumstances, but are not
true simulations. They are games that simulate certain conditions.

Physical Experiential Games

Physical experiential games require the participants to carry out some
type of physical activity. The learning focus is literally on the physical
feeling and its effects. Such games can be held outdoors and incorporate running, yelling, and making lots of noise. They can be held
indoors and give people a chance to move, stretch, and walk about.
They might require participants to do something simple like "close
your eyes, and keeping your eyes closed, pick up a pen or pencil and
write your name, address, and phone number on a piece of paper. Fold
up the paper and drop it into the hat that is being passed around." Or
physical experiential games can be more complicated such as in a "trust
walk," where participants are blindfolded, and holding hands and
forming a long line, they must allow themselves to be led along an intricate path with information about the path being passed along verbally
from person to person.

The names in the hat, in the first game above, are drawn and read
by participants. Any person whose information is correctly read wins a
prize. Then the class debriefs what it feels like not to be able to use their
vision in this simple task. What happened to their other senses? What
difficulties did they encounter? In the second example, the "trust
walk," participants experience what it is like to be at various points
along the information chain, never knowing exactly what is happening,
right before, or even as it happens.

Graham Roberts-Phelps has a physical experiential game called "Running Blind" in his collection of *Health and Safety Games for Trainers,* which has some participants leading other blindfolded participants through obstacles and finally carrying a glass of water. He suggests using this game as "a way of getting home the message that wearing eye protection and using safety guards are very good ideas."[15]

The purpose of the more physical experiential games is to provide participants with an immediate physical happening that they can then consider, analyze, and discuss. It's one thing to know that people should wear eye protection in certain areas of a production facility; it's quite another thing to feel what loss of eyesight would be like!

In another example, small groups stand in circles holding hands and, without letting go of hands, try to pass a hula hoop from person to person around the circle and back to where it started. The first group to get the hula hoop around the complete circle in less than three minutes wins a prize. The experience that is focused on in such a game might be the feelings of always being part of the group, literally linked to one another, holding hands with someone you don't know well, and being somewhat dependent on them. Other related experiences could include being trapped in place, not being able to use your full resources (hands), and having to depend on others and their behavior in order to win.

I've also used the hula hoop game to illustrate the power of motivation and meaningful rewards. Just to win the game is somewhat motivating, but to win a sack of chocolate candy is even more motivating. By the way, the most powerful motivator I have found (apart from money, of course) is a promise of "getting out of class early." I try to convince myself that these are busy people who value the gift of time, and not people who just want to escape my class!

There are pros and cons to using physical experiential games, of course. They can be quite effective, particularly with participants who are very sensory oriented in their learning styles. The impact of actually experiencing a phenomenon is hard to match in other types of games and activities. However, the use of physical activity brings problems of mobility, body size, physical contact, and even the potential of injury— all of which need to be considered and addressed in some way.

Activity Experiential Games

These games have the participants completing some type of task relevant to the course content; but, as they carry out the task in order to win the game, they encounter difficulties and undergo different experiences. The activity may be the main focus as the game begins, but the experiences of the participants are the main focus of the debriefing and the key learnings for the game. A good example of this type of experiential game is *Diversity Bingo*.[16] At first *Diversity Bingo* appears to be a content-focused matrix game—cover five squares and get a "bingo"—but, as the game unfolds, participants begin to experience their own perceptions and assumptions about others in the group and eventually may experience the perceptions and assumptions that other people have about them as well.

As participants mix and mingle, trying get a "bingo" by covering five squares down, across, or diagonally, they look for people to sign their card who fit the categories. As they try to find "a person over 60 years of age," "a single parent," "a person of Asian heritage," "a person who is a veteran," and so forth, they begin to feel reluctant to ask certain questions. They are surprised when people keep asking them to sign for a particular category. They feel annoyed that they are only asked to sign for one category, over and over, but not for the other four categories that also apply to them. These feelings of reluctance, surprise, and annoyance must be debriefed with sensitivity and the learning unfolded with care. The real learning in this game includes "how it feels to be perceived so narrowly" and "how easily we make assumptions about one another."

Another example of an activity experiential game is one that uses the Interel electronic carpet maze.[17] This 8 foot by 6 foot, forty-eight square matrix carpet can be programmed so that some of the squares beep when you step on them and some do not. Thus, you can create a maze of nonbeeping squares across the carpet. The carpet comes with a games manual and a variety of suggested uses.

One of my favorite uses of the electronic carpet maze is a game in which, in order to win, members of a team must meet a number of challenges presented through various rules in order to get team members across the carpet one-by-one without setting off any beeps. After participants work hard at this team-building activity, find the path across the carpet, and begin to get players across without a beep, I change the path. The various feelings and reactions the players demonstrate in handling this change is the real learning focus of the game. Yes, they learn about working together, group communication, and many other team behaviors as well from the general activity; but the experiencing of "real time change" is the major focus and where much of the learning is centered.

Improv games are another type of activity experiential games. In his book, *Improvisation, Inc.,* Robert Lowe states that, "improvisation can be experienced as a method for creating perspective shifts"[18] and many improv games do just that. Based on improvisational comedy theater principles and techniques, improv games and activities are often used as part of creativity and innovation training to get the creative juices going. In fact, Alain Rostain of Creative Advantage has developed a set of improvisational activities called *Juicers*[19] that, in addition to getting creative juices flowing, can also be used to raise a group's energy level, to improve group communication skills, and to accomplish various other goals.

A game called "Quick Draw,"[20] which is available at Creative Advantage.com, has players working in pairs to draw a picture, adding one line at a time, not communicating verbally, alternating back and forth until one player hesitates. When a player hesitates the drawing is done. This continues until all pairs have completed three drawings. Through the debriefing, it becomes apparent how well the players worked together and how good the finished products are. Players literally experience a different way of doing something; some experience discomfort working with a partner at first, others experience their need for control and how it feels to let go of that.

Although activity experiential games have people up and moving around and doing things, they do not have as many issues of mobility, body size, physical contact, and potential injury as some of the physical experiential games. However, they will often require additional space and/or large open areas that may be difficult to find. With very large groups of people, the trainer may need assistance in monitoring and facilitating such games.

Experiential Simulation Games

Simulation games are based on models of reality. Players in a simulation game experience what it is like to do something. They are not experiencing it "in reality," but the simulation game produces feelings similar to those experienced in reality. Ken Jones describes a true simulation as "a classroom event which has two essential characteristics: 1. The participants have functional roles—survivor, journalist, judge, fashion designer, prime minister" and "2. Sufficient information is provided on an issue or a problem—memos, maps, newspaper items, documents, materials—to enable the participants to function as professionals."[21]

Jones and others make a distinction between a simulation game and a real simulation. "Unlike games, where everyone has the role of player with a duty to try to win, simulations require 'professional ethics.' A well-designed simulation provides enough key facts to allow the participants to function professionally."[22] But a true simulation does not have winners and losers as such, and it often has players beginning under unequal conditions and encountering different challenges and circumstances.

Sivasailam Thiagarajan (Thiagi), a pioneer in simulation gaming, defines a simulation game as "a game in which the procedures and play materials reflect real-world processes and products."[23] In his various writings and games materials, Thiagi gives a number of reasons for using simulation games including the fact that "well-designed simulation games reflect relevant dimensions of the real world and, hence, ensure rapid transfer of training to the workplace."[24] He also says that simulation games can reduce economic and emotional risks associated with on-the-job training in interpersonal skills.

Simulation games are usually much shorter and less complex that simulation events. The goals of the two are also different. Simulation events stress an experience that mirrors real life as closely as possible and presents the player with events and choices as real as possible; thus learning comes from immersion in a detailed, life-like experience. The simulation game, however, has as its goal the reflecting of the relevant dimensions of the real-world situation, but in an encapsulated form that stresses the action that produces the insight for learning.

There is a vast array of simulation games and activities on the market today. The quality and effectiveness of these products can vary greatly. Again, it is helpful to ask other trainers about their experiences with simulation games. If there is a particular game or a specific designer of such games that other trainers recommend, that is a great starting place. Also, many simulation games, and other experiential games as well, are sold via "participant workbooks" and an instructor's manual. So, you may want to purchase the instructor's manual and one workbook for inspection before purchasing large numbers of the workbooks.

Stranded in the Himalayas[25] by Lorraine L. Ukens is a good example of an experiential simulation game using participant workbooks with a leader's manual. This particular simulation game uses survival in the Himalayan Mountains as a theme to have work teams or groups experience differences between individual decision making and group consensus. The game can also provide immediate feedback to the team on how well they perform as a team regarding such issues as decision making, problem solving, and teamwork in general. This type of simulation game takes from one to two hours to play, depending on the length and depth of the debriefing.

One of my favorite experiential simulation games is *BARNGA,* a simulation game of cultural clashes, designed by Thiagi. Thiagi refers to *BARNGA* as a "metaphorical simulation game" that "reflects a few selected real-world elements in an abstract, simplified fashion."[26] Basically, this experiential simulation game places participants in a situation where they experience the shock of realizing that in spite of many surface similarities, there are subtle underlying differences among them that are causing problems.

One of the many attractive features of *BARNGA,* and similar "metaphorical simulation games," is that they can provide a very rich learning experience in a very short time. Such experiential games can teach principles and bring about insights; learning experiences are shared by all the participants and can be referred to throughout the rest of the training program. In addition, the sheer energy created through such a game can flow through the entire training program.

3. Content and Experiential Frame Games

A frame game is a generic game template. It is designed for use with different types of content. Steve Sugar writes that, "The concept of frame, like that of a picture frame, is that part of the game that is open to 'load' or fill-in with your material—the content or information that you wish to present."[27] Thiagi explains it this way, "A frame game is an activity that is deliberately designed to permit the easy unloading of old content and the insertion of new content. It is a generic game template that permits the instant design of new games."[28]

Most frame games are content focused. For trainers wanting to design games to fit their specific content, frame games are often a good place to start. The frame or template is purchased and includes instructions for using your own subject matter within the frame and guidelines for effectively conducting and debriefing the game.

Content-focused frame games are directed toward subject content; the games have been designed specifically to enhance and expedite the learning of the particular content that is put into them. The trainer has the dual role of designer and facilitator. The trainer provides the content that goes into the generic frame, and then the trainer facilitates and debriefs the game. The major learning, however, comes from focusing on and interacting with the subject matter. Content-focused frame games can come in any of the categories discussed under content-focused games earlier in this chapter.

Most of the compendiums of games and activities available in the marketplace do not include frame games. However, a few of them do, but often do not advertise that they do so. I'm not sure if this is because they do not recognize the distinction between frame games and non-frame games, or have simply chosen not to make note of the two types.

One mix of content-focused games and frame games that I found in my frequent big game hunting expeditions for this book was Elyssebeth Leigh and Jeff Kinder's *Learning through Fun and Games*.[29] This book contains games and activities designed, tested, and determined as highly effective during study for the Bachelor of Education in Adult Education at the University of Technology, Sydney. Forty games and simulations are included in the publication, six of which they label "frame games."

One of Leigh and Kinders' frame games is called "Where Is It?" and has a sort of "treasure hunt" format in which participants must find items and/or get questions answered in a large area such as a factory, a hotel, or a hospital. Leigh and Kinder present the structure or format of the game, resources that are needed, how to conduct the game and the debrief, and so on; but the actual items or questions to be "found" are put into the "frame" by the trainer using the frame game.

Steve Sugar's *Quizo*[30] is an excellent example of a content-focused frame game. It uses the Bingo format with the trainer asking a series of questions. For every question answered correctly, players cover a space on the game sheet. This format is particularly good for reviewing specific content, content that the trainer supplies. Sugar also presents a step-by-step procedure for designing board games that is virtually a "frame" for board games in the article, "Customizing a Board Game with Your Classroom Material" in *ASTD's 1993 Handbook of Instructional Technology.*[31]

The most prolific source of frame games, both content-focused and experiential, is Thiagi. Some of his games include generic game templates, sample procedures and content, and various reproducible material; others use a generic game but provide variations that allow the game to be adapted in different ways. For example, his game *Triangles*[32] is basically a simulation game that explores factors associated with planning and implementing new work processes. However, the game kit comes with information on how to modify the game to highlight other themes such as employee involvement and quality control, therefore, moving in the direction of an experiential frame game.

There are many advantages for using frame games; the major one being that "design time" is minimal. Someone else has tested and perfected the format. You don't need to run developmental tests, pilot it with different groups, and finally modify it. All you have to do is insert your own content, and it's ready to go! Frame games are great when your course content is too unique or specific for the general games that are available. Frame games can be inexpensive, in that they are not for just one training program or one subject. They can be used for a variety of courses and occasions and can address many issues and topics. The problems with frame games are often caused by the trainer; that is, the trainer may use material that really isn't a good fit with the design of the frame or may make mistakes in the process that hinder the effectiveness of the game.

Final Thoughts

I'm sure it seems as if we have covered an endless array of training games and activities that are available in the training and development marketplace; but in truth, we have barely scratched the surface. After twenty years as a professional trainer, facilitator, and presenter, I thought I had a pretty good grasp of what was available in the world of training games. But, as I journeyed through that world, I made some new discoveries and so will you. There is one huge area that we did not explore—the flourishing terrain of electronic training games. That booming territory is covered in Chapter 4.

In a Nutshell

To facilitate reviewing the vast array of interactive training games available in the marketplace today, I have divided them into four categories: content-focused games where the learning is focused on the material content of the game; experiential games where the actual physical experience is the focus of the learning; and content-focused frame games and experiential frame games where the template or structure of the game is provided and the trainer must supply the actual content. There are many different categories of content-focused games, such as paper-and-pencil games, card games, board games, artistic and acting games, and a variety of others. Experiential games include physical experiential, activity experiential, and simulation games. Although most frame games are content focused, there are some simulation games that are frame games.

Notes

1. John Newstrom and Edward Scannell, *Games Trainers Play* (New York: McGraw-Hill, 1980).

2. Ibid.

3. Graham Roberts-Phelps, *Health and Safety Games for Trainers* (London: Gower Publishing, 1999).

4. Susan El-Shamy and Gayle Stuebe, *The Performance Improvement Pack: Situations for Developing Feedback Skills* (Bloomington, IN: Action Pack Learning Card Series, Advancement Strategies, Inc., 1995).

5. Susan El-Shamy and Gayle Stuebe, *An Instructor's Guide to Action Packs* (Bloomington, IN: Action Pack Learning Card Series, Advancement Strategies, Inc., 1991).

6. Joshua Kerievsky, *Design Patterns Playing Cards* (San Francisco, CA: Industrial Logic, 2000).

7. Ken Jones, *Simulations: A Handbook for Teachers and Trainers* (London: Kogan-Page, 1995).

8. Steve Sugar, "Customizing a Board Game with Your Classroom Material," in *The ASTD Handbook of Instructional Technology* (New York: McGraw Hill, 1993).

9. David Parlett, *The Oxford History of Board Games* (London: Oxford University Press, 1999).

10. The Lead Group International, *The Customer Journey, The Sales Journey,* and *The Leadership Journey* (Lilburn, GA: The Lead Group International, 1997).

11. Gayle Stuebe and Susan El-Shamy, *Card Games for Developing Teams,* (London: Gower Publishing, and Amhurst, MA: HRD Press, 1999).

12. Gayle Stuebe and Susan El-Shamy, *Card Games for Developing Service* (London: Gower Publishing, 2000).

13. Graham Roberts-Phelps, *Health and Safety Games.*

14. Jeff Stibbard, *Training Games—from the Inside* (Australia: Business & Professional Publishing Pty Limited, 1998).

15. Graham Roberts-Phelps, *Health and Safety Games*.

16. Susan El-Shamy and Gayle Stuebe, *Diversity Bingo* (Bloomington, IN: Advancement Strategies, Inc., and San Francisco, CA: Pfieffer/Jossey-Bass, 1990).

17. Interel, *The Electronic Maze*, (San Francisco, CA: Interel, Inc., 1991).

18. Robert Lowe, *Improvisation, Inc.—Harnessing Spontaneity to Engage People and Groups* (San Francisco, CA: Jossey-Bass/ Pfeiffer, 2000).

19. Alain Rostain, *Juicers* (San Francisco, CA: Creative Advantage, 2000).

20. Creative Advantage, *Quick Draw*, creativeadvantage.com, 2000.

21. Ken Jones, *Simulations*.

22. Ibid.

23. Sivasailam Thiagarajan, *Triangles* (Amherst, MA: HRD Press, 1994).

24. Sivasailam Thiagarajan, *Cash Games* (Amherst, MA: HRD Press, 1994).

25. Lorraine L. Ukens, *Stranded in the Himalayas* (San Francisco, CA: Jossey-Bass/Pfeiffer, 1998).

26. www.thiagi.com

27. Steve Sugar, "Customizing a Board Game."

28. www.thiagi.com

29. Elyssebeth Leigh and Jeff Kinder, *Learning through Fun and Games*, (Australia: McGraw Hill, 1999).

30. Steve Sugar, *Quizo Game System* (Kensington, MD: The Game Group, 1992).

31. Steve Sugar, "Customizing a Board Game."

32. Sivasailam Thiagarajan, *Triangles*.

My first encounter with an "e-game" was in 1981 when I became obsessed with Pac-Man. We were living in Cairo, Egypt, at the time, and I had brought the plastic, battery-operated mini-version of the arcade game back with me after a trip to the States. For the kids to play with. Which they did for a while. Then I began to play—morning, noon, and nighttime too. Game after game, I played and played. I began to develop a callous on the thumb of my right hand. I dreamed of little yellow dot-gobbling creatures, pursued by blue ghosts. I discussed dot-gobbling strategies with members of my car pool. And then one day, it happened. I ran out of C batteries. There was a shortage in Egypt then and by the time we got our hands on some, the spell was broken and I set the game aside.

4

IT'S HOW YOU PLAY THE GAME

ELECTRONIC TRAINING GAMES

Electronic training games are changing the "how" of training games. "E-learning" is the largest area of growth in the training and development marketplace today and one of the largest areas of growth on the Internet. As a market sector, e-learning goes far beyond training and development to include "educational content creation and delivery in K-12, colleges and universities, at home and in corporate environments."[1] The total education industry in the United States is "some $772 billion strong and is the second largest sector of the U.S. economy next to healthcare."[2] If you pause at the sidelines of this emerging e-learning industry right now, you can watch the players of the learning game scurry and scramble to assemble those first superhighways into E-City. The term of choice for these thoroughfares is "learning portals": consolidated access doorways to total learning services, not just learning content services, but knowledge management and learning technologies as well.

The incredible energy, the staggering amounts of money and the continual merging, acquiring, and forming of strategic alliances within the e-learning industry is astounding. In an article in *e-learning* magazine entitled "E-learning in the New Economy," Michael Moe, director of Global Growth Stock Research and a managing director at Merrill Lynch, writes, "Technology is the drive of the New Economy, and human capital is its fuel. . . . While the future possibilities of the knowledge economy look both exciting and, at the same time, daunting, the transformation to a knowledge economy is now evident."[3]

Moe goes on later in the same article to suggest that the Information Revolution is really the Knowledge Revolution and that the "Internet is to the Knowledge Revolution what the railroad was to the Industrial Revolution." He sees the Internet as having the potential "to 'democratize' knowledge and learning, increasing the access, lowering the cost and improving the quality."[4]

As e-learning becomes the fuel of choice for the knowledge worker on the information highway, traditional suppliers of training and development must produce superior quantities of this new fuel, or be left behind. However, some of the early attempts at online learning and electronic training resources have been spotty at best. While it is quite possible to put games and interactive activities into online training courses, it appears to be happening in only a limited way, as yet. Evidently, in the mad race to get to market first, too many online courses merely became pages of former participant guides pasted to a screen. These uninspired courses require participants to point and click or endlessly scroll away through boring page after boring page.

Clark N. Quinn, director of Cognitive Systems at Knowledge-Planet.com, wrote in a paper not long ago, "How do we move educational technology from the page-turning applications that have given CAL (computer assisted learning) a bad name to an environment that helps retain the inherent interest of learning? The ideal would be an activity that intrinsically 'engages' the learner, and leads them through an interactive experience that enhances their ability to solve problems."[5]

Quinn goes on to suggest that, at least for cognitive skills, learning approaches are converging on a model that includes motivating the learning by demonstrating the practical applications and importance of the knowledge, providing a conceptual description of the skill, demonstrating the application of the knowledge to practical problems, providing practice opportunities with support in the form of scaffolding, and facilitating transfer through guided reflection on the activity to integrate the practical issues with the underlying conception.[6] Quinn suggests that "with good design and good guidelines for support, computer games can be engaging and educationally effective. . . . the problem is to educate the game designers to make the effort to design challenging games that are based on valuable cognitive skills." Players learn the things needed to play games. Therefore games should be designed to require the things we wish to learn. "To effectively engage learning, we can and should make learning engaging."[7]

I believe that is happening. Yes, there is plenty of really bad, boring e-learning going on, but there are also some excellent products out there and more can be expected in the very near future as the e-learning revolution rolls along. In this chapter we will take a look at some of the games appearing within that revolution and project a few possibilities for e-games of the near future.

What Is E-Learning and Where Do Electronic Games Fit In?

The American Society for Training and Development (ASTD) defines e-learning as being "anything delivered, enabled, or mediated by electronic technology for the explicit purpose of learning."[8] This includes online learning, Web-based training, and computer-based training of all types. In a presentation to the ASTD 2000 Conference in Dallas, Texas, Brandon Hall, a leading independent researcher in e-learning, asserted that "By the year 2002, it is predicted that over $96 billion dollars worth of training will go online and that somewhere between 40% and

60% of U.S. employee training will occur online."[9] Electronic training games are a vital tool within this e-learning bonanza.

Electronic training games are just as useful and important a training tool for e-learning as they are for "c-learning," classroom learning, perhaps even more so. Just as electronic training has increased rapidly in the last few years, so has the number and variety of electronic training games. Electronic training games are training games played on and/or with electronic devices, including battery-operated devices. These could be computers, televisions, hand-held game machines, pagers and messaging devices, palm pilots, and video game machines. Delivery mediums can include telephones, the Internet, Intranets, CDROMs, and videos.

Another significant transformation taking place as more and more training occurs outside the traditional classroom is the role of the trainer. When it comes to electronic training, you may find that your training activities fall into one of three categories: designer-developer of e-training; facilitator of training programs that combine e-learning and c-learning; or virtual facilitator. That is, you will design e-learning programs that may include e-games; or you will do training that combines electronic learning and regular classroom learning with games in both arenas; or you will facilitate e-learning through the Internet, Intranet, e-mail, and/or other long-distance means and that can include facilitating e-games. In any of these "e-trainer roles," you will be using training games to engage the learner and reinforce the learning.

Electronic training games are appearing throughout the electronic learning literature and the growing technology-based training marketplace. Let's use our matrix again to help sort and identify these various electronic training games (Figure 4.1).

The games themselves can be assigned to the same categories as their nonelectronic counterparts: content-focused, experiential, or content and experiential frame games. If the learning occurs primarily by the learner interacting with the content material of the game, then it is a content-focused game. Some of the subcategories may need different terminology. For example, a paper-and-pencil game may become a screen-and-mouse game, and most of the experiential games will be of the simulation game variety; but the major learning still comes from the content or the experience, or both. Let's take a look at some of

Training Games Matrix		
Learning occurs through:	Trainer is required to:	
	Facilitate given content	Insert content and facilitate
the learner's interaction with the content	1. Content-Focused Games	3. Content-Focused Frame Games
the learner's physical experiencing of the content	2. Experiential Games	4. Experiential Frame Games

FIGURE 4.1

these e-games that you are now, or soon will be, playing, designing, and facilitating.

Content-Focused E-Games

Content-focused electronic training games are games and activities that make use of computers, the Internet or Intranet, or other electronic devices and delivery systems, and in which the subject content of the game is the focal point of the learning. These games are designed specifically to enhance and expedite the learning of a particular subject matter content. Participants or players of the games follow given rules in a given context and employ the paraphernalia used by that game to move toward achieving a set goal that determines winning. These games are the electronic equivalents of paper-and-pencil games such as timed true-and-false quizzes, lists of items that need to be transformed in some way, puzzles that illustrate learning points, fill-in-the-blank review games, matrix games, and so on and so forth.

When electronic content-focused games are used in a classroom-based training program, they can be assigned as pre-work or homework, or they can be used during the class. When used during class, the instructor gives individual participants or small groups of participants assignments to be carried out by playing some type of interactive computer game, by accessing a Web site that contains a game that they play, or requiring the use of a computer and/or the Internet to obtain information needed to win the game. Participants often play the games at computers in other locations outside the classroom, either by using CDROMs or accessing Web sites, then returning to the classroom setting to debrief and discuss the learning. It is also possible for the instructor to use a computer, the Internet, or an Intranet, to access a game and project it onto a large screen in the classroom and have the class play as a whole. These types of games are, of course, further enhanced by the fact that they can be facilitated and immediately debriefed by an experienced trainer who can enhance and reinforce the learning.

Electronic game playing can add much needed variety and involvement to participant learning activities in the classroom and is relatively inexpensive, flexible, and "trainer friendly." Disadvantages of computer and Web-accessed training games in the classroom include the problem of having access to enough computers, the "travel time and distance" between the training room and the location of the computers if they are not in the same room, and attending to the problems of technologically disadvantaged participants. But the advantages of learner engagement in well-designed electronic games may very well outweigh the disadvantages.

Training games can also be incorporated into the design and delivery of electronic training courses, either for Web-based, Internet or Intranet delivery, or CBT (computer-based training) use. Certainly designers of "Web-based training" are aware of the need for more interactivity in electronic training programs. William Horton, training design consultant, has a Web site dedicated to the content of his book, *Designing Web-Based Training*,[10] (www.designingwbt.com). His Web site offers not only great advice for designing Web-based training, and lots of examples, but also advocates the use of games to make training more appealing, to let people discover patterns and relationship for themselves, and to provide practice to hone skills and modify behavior.

For example, in *The Crime Scene Game,* the teaching of interviewing skills is covered in the context of a police investigation. "Learners are assigned the task of interviewing a witness to a bank robbery. The game provides the player with choices that affect the course of the game. At any point learners can try to solve the mystery. Most feedback is provided by events in the game."[11] Players in this game receive a score based on the proficiency with which they solved the mystery; they also receive a critique of their actions with comments on each action.

The Diet Game is another example from Horton's Web site. This game has players ordering restaurant meals to meet specific dietary requirements; it allows learners to make changes to different parameters in a complex system and see their results immediately. Players can keep tweaking and tuning their answers until they succeed. It's not as easy as it sounds; it took me seven attempts to get it right. I just kept underestimating the fat content of certain favorite foods!

More information, advice, examples, and illustrations can be found on Horton's professional Web site, www.horton.com. The content of a Horton presentation, *Games@Work,* is available on this Web site and offers an overview of the value of adding games to online training and presents information on what types of games can best be used for what types of learning. He suggests that Web-based training should consider arcade-style games to test and hone recognition and reaction skills; adventure games to discover concepts, principles, and patterns; simulations to use when it is too dangerous or expensive to learn on the job; word games to teach vocabulary; and quiz-show games to test knowledge.[12] This presentation also includes some excellent advice on convincing management that games promote learning.

Unfortunately, far too few Web-based training programs make use of this type of engaging game playing and it's difficult to find out which those few are. Short of actually taking the course, it is almost impossible to know exactly what the contents of any online training course will include, even if you can preview some of it. Many of the new "learning portals" and e-learning providers like *Click2Learn.com* have sample offers like "take a free online training course," that you can take advantage of. How representative the "free course" is of all the courses available is hard to say, but it is a free online course!

Usually the purveyors of online learning courses have means by which you can inspect some of the content before purchasing a course. Often, however, you are only able to access information about course objectives and what is covered, but not particularly *how* it is covered. Some descriptions will include comments like "interactive exercises help you practice new skills," and use words like "match, select, and identify" in their course objectives. So, there may or may not be games included.

There are online training courses that have reviews included in their information, much like Amazon.com does for its books. The reviews may be from users or from "experts" or both. One helpful resource in perusing information about online learning programs is *Lguide.com,* a Web site that rates and reviews online courses and often has available comparative reviews of a variety of online courses on a particular topic. Although these reviews are excellent and really helpful to the seeker of effective online learning, reference to games is seldom found. Now, unfortunately, this probably indicates the absence of "real games" in most online learning courses, but, as courses improve, as they surely must, the positive, engaging, and reinforcing aspects of games will become more utilized.

Many of the "interactive exercises" that help learners practice new skills in these online courses could easily be made into games, just as classroom activities can often be turned into games. By adding rules, time limits, challenge, competition, and perhaps a story line of some sort, a mildly involving activity could become a highly involving game. Again, many of the games that could be used in electronic training programs are the electronic counterparts of paper-and-pencil content-focused learning games, such as quizzes, puzzles, fill-in-the-blank, and matrix games. Variations of card games and board games could also be incorporated into an electronic format to reinforce the practicing and refining of participant knowledge.

Such games could be designed for the learner to compete with the game itself, or mechanisms could be added to track the top scores of other players who have played the game, much like video and pinball games that record the initials of high-scoring players. Some games could even be designed for several people to play simultaneously and see one another's scores as they play. Game playing can add much needed variety and involvement to e-learning activities and it is relatively inexpensive to do so.

Experiential Electronic Games

Experiential electronic games are those in which the major learning takes place through the actual physical experiencing of the player. Learning occurs by doing, by feeling, and by experiencing. The focus of the learning is on the activity being carried out, not on specific content. The content can add additional learning, but the experience is the focus of the game and the learning.

Web quest games are a good example of experiential e-games used in classroom training. Web quest games are designed to help participants learn to use the Internet. Players are given questions and URLs, "Web addresses," as sources of information to find the answers; they have rules and time limits or deadline dates and are sometimes played in teams. The players go online and search the Internet for information to answer the questions in the game. This type of electronic game is considered an experiential game in that the content is not the primary focus of the learning, although it can certainly add to the learning. The primary learning comes from the experience of using the Internet and the World Wide Web.

E-Sims in Training Programs

E-Sims is a term being applied to electronic simulation games. Such games can be a part of classroom learning; they can be incorporated into e-learning courses; and they can occasionally be used as stand-alone electronic game-based learning. Presently, e-Sims are most often found as a component of standard classroom training, both in the business world and in higher education. Such electronic simulation games may be utilized as pre-work, homework, in-class activities, and/or as ongoing learning activities used in conjunction with a series of training programs. Many of today's business school programs make use of electronic simulations, often having numerous program courses linked with a central ongoing management simulation.

In a presentation to the North American Simulation and Games Association (NASAGA) in the fall of 2000, Dr. Owen Hall of Pepperdine University explained that there is an increasing demand for a more customized approach to learning including a demand for "global perspective, distance learning, integrated learning experiences, and students to serve as co-producers of learning."[13] Dr. Hall pointed out that electronic experiential simulation games are becoming a staple in many types of "distance learning" situations within graduate schools, adult continuing education programs, and corporate training programs as well. Such programs will often make available business simulation games along with access to industry online tours, case studies, chat rooms, self-testing, and diagnostic services. This format of a variety of online training options, including e-sims, is becoming more and more common as higher numbers of working adults enroll in business school graduate programs and are creating a need for "distance learning" options and "customized learning services."

At the same NASAGA conference, Dr. Scott Fallows, the director of the Acadia Centre for Virtual Learning Environments at Acadia University in Nova Scotia, Canada, described the opportunities provided by virtual learning environments (which I'm including under the category of simulation games) as "requiring the learner to solve problems in order to acquire knowledge and skills; to make choices; to safely experience failure and learn from mistakes; and to receive just-in-time expert knowledge/coaching."[14] These "virtual learning environments" can be presented on CDROMs, and then combined with face-to-face classroom learning. A Web site can be included where participants work online in groups as a virtual team practicing new skills and discussing their views online with other "virtual team members." Fallows describes this as "an asynchronous environment monitored by a trained facilitator."

Further benefits that Fallows assigns to such virtual learning environments include:

- the learner being able to control the learning process thus increasing motivation and task persistence;

- the accommodation of a wide range of learning styles;

- the requirement for the learner to integrate a complex knowledge base that can be used when confronted with a novel situation;

- the engagement of the learner through the storytelling aspects of the simulation.[15]

Dr. Fallows presented excerpts from a clever, involving "virtual learning environment" on team building that simulated a rescue team canoe trip. The game gave players options on solving problems in a team environment and allowed players to make mistakes and learn from those mistakes. Another helpful element in the simulation was the ability to access a "coach" for helpful advice.

While well-designed e-sims can be extremely effective, they do have a major disadvantage in that they can be expensive and time-consuming to design and develop. Time and costs for a good e-sim can range anywhere from four months and thousands of dollars (as did Dr. Fallow's canoe trip simulation), to a year or two and hundreds of thousands of dollars! But once created, most e-sims are rather easily updated, adjusted, and modified. In fact, if created with the intention of becoming a "frame game," the initial design and development costs could be distributed over a number of subsequent electronic simulation games.

Content and Experiential Electronic Frame Games

An electronic frame game is a generic electronic game template designed to be used with different types of content and that permits the instant design of new games. These game templates can be utilized to design electronic games (1) that can be used in the classroom and facilitated by the instructor, (2) that can be inserted into electronic training courses and used by learners who take the course, or (3) that can be distributed directly to learners as an individual, stand-alone training mechanism. This is a category of electronic games that is just beginning to grow, but I'm sure more games and more categories are being devised as I write.

Software for Facilitator-Led Classroom Games

An interesting variety of software for facilitator-led electronic classroom learning games is available on the marketplace. Like many popular nonelectronic classroom games, these electronic learning games are often based on popular game-show formats such as *Jeopardy, Tic Tac Toe,* and *Who Wants to be a Millionaire?* These games are within software programs that the trainer puts into a classroom computer, projects onto a screen, and then uses with the class in a game-show format. Players can navigate through the game with on-screen buttons or keyboard commands.

There are also wired and wireless buzzer systems available that can be used with some of these games. For example, *Gameshow Pro3*[16] from Learning Ware has wired and wireless buzzer lockout systems that can be integrated with the games. When a participant or a team rings in, the software automatically responds by playing a distinctive sound and highlights that team's scorebox on the screen. All the other players or teams are then automatically locked out.

Most of these games are content-focused frame games that allow trainers to easily input their own content and create an unlimited number of classroom games. The learning comes from the player's interaction with the content material. Many of these electronic game shells have a standard configuration that is designed for content review activities in a facilitator-led learning environment. But such formats can also be used for introducing new material, practicing the use of new material, and testing knowledge. These game programs can also be used by individual learners and self-administered.

Pricing and/or licensing for these software programs for facilitator-led classroom games range greatly depending on a number of factors such as how many games are included, what type of "buzz-in" options are included, how many computers will be using the game (10, 200, unlimited), and what systems are required for use. All game packages seem to be available for PC Windows 3.1/95/98/NT and some are also available for us Mac users as well. Most also require at least 8MB of Ram, 4 to 20 MB of hard drive space, and both video and sound cards. Prices range from $400.00 for a single copy up to $3,000.00 for unlimited numbers of computers.[17]

A few final words about e-learning software game-show formats. When administered and facilitated well, these games can be extremely energizing and effective in reinforcing learning. They are fun, involving, and very potent learning tools. Most of the companies who market these products have examples that you can view on their Web sites and many offer samples that you can download. (See the Appendix on Web sites.) It is also possible to license some of these products for inclusion in e-learning courses that you design. About the only caveat that I can offer in regard to such games is to be careful that you are truly using these games to reinforce your major learning objectives and that you are not devoting inordinate amounts of time to playing these games just because they are so much fun!

Computer Game Shell Software

Computer game shell software programs contain game frames or templates designed around familiar training games such as puzzles, timed true-and-false quizzes, lists of items that need to be transformed in some way, fill-in-the-blank, matrix games, and so on. These software programs usually come with one or more game frames, sample games, player manuals, and a game designer's manual. Once such game shells are in the hands of an experienced, creative trainer, putting them to use in your own online learning events should not only be easy, it should be quite enjoyable as well!

Thiagi has a set of Computer Game Shells that includes ten different ready-to-use computer games, sample games, and player and designer manuals, and is reasonably priced. Unfortunately, it is presently available only for PCs. This set of game shells comes with permission to "distribute your games royalty-free," which is further explained as "distribute your games freely to employees in your organization without paying expensive royalty or licensing fees. Once you have created a game, you may pass it out to employees on diskette. . . ."[18] If these game shells are to be used in games that will become part of online learning programs marketed outside your company, it would be wise to check into the need to license them.

As I mentioned earlier in the section on electronic experiential simulation games, some e-sims have been designed in such a way that they can be modified and, perhaps, if the original game is used as a frame, they could be adapted into simulations addressing different content. As e-training becomes more and more common, the need for electronic frame games should grow proportionately and clever designers will undoubtedly respond to that need.

Electronic Game-Based Training

There is another e-learning phenomenon appearing on the horizon that has both great appeal and great promise: "electronic game-based training." In electronic game-based training, the game is the medium of instruction. To take the course is to play the game. Or, perhaps, the reverse is more appropriate: Playing the game is taking the course. In reality, of course, there is no course; there is only learning of subject matter and/or skills.

When proponents of e-leaning speak of "the death of the course," they are referring to a number of changing paradigms in regard to learning and training, such as anytime, anyplace access to information and the "democratization" of knowledge and learning. But there will also be the addition of entirely new modes of learning—well, new to the fields of education, training, and development, anyway.

E-mail Games

E-mail games are fairly low tech, but can be effective in gaining participation from players who live in different geographical regions. They are a very effective way of brainstorming, information gathering, and building consensus. In e-mail games, the facilitator and the players communicate by sending electronic messages. Most e-mail games are played in rounds and can take anywhere from a few days to a few weeks to complete. Most e-mail games also need to be tied into a Web site where instructions, generated ideas, and results can be posted and updated easily.

E-mail games are content focused, with much of the content supplied by the learners. E-mail games require someone to initiate and manage the game. This can be anyone who wants the game to happen for whatever reason and a trainer can certainly take on that role. The initiator or trainer's role in an e-mail game is to introduce and set up the game, manage the game (no small task as you will see!), and debrief when it is over. To illustrate, it could be a brainstorming game on orienting new employees, dealing with stress on the job, or enlivening a computer training class. With a fairly broad topic, the trainer may want to add categories of responses. For example, if you were gathering ideas for enlivening a computer training class, you might use categories like: the classroom, the instructional material, the exercises, student-to-student interactions, and student-instructor interactions. The instructor might also generate a few examples of ideas to serve as a model.

E-mail games are usually conducted in three to six rounds, although they can certainly be designed for any number of rounds. They are sent to a set number of participants with directions and schedules. The setting of time schedules for the game depends on the number of players, the complexity of the game, how far away the players are in geographical terms, and how much time will be required of the trainer to process the responses from the players. So, the directions for the overall game are sent out to all players along with the instructions for the first round, which usually solicits a set number of ideas. In our example above, we would send out an e-mail introducing the game to say twenty players and for the first round, ask them to submit four ideas on how to enliven a computer training class using any of the given categories, and to do so by a certain time.

Different types of games handle the arriving ideas in different ways, but basically the ideas are grouped and listed. There are various means of adding gaming elements to the activity. Points can be given for each idea submitted. Judges can be used to award points for ideas, giving so many points for the best, the next best, and so forth. Peer evaluation is often used and ideas are ranked or the top amount is chosen. Certain criteria can be included into the game instructions and applied to the ideas by peer evaluators or judges and points awarded accordingly.

Another method is to have all ideas listed on the Web site; and, in round two, participants vote for the best ideas. Some games also have participants predict what they think will be chosen as the top three or top ten ideas. Winners are those who most closely predict the outcomes, those whose ideas are ranked among the top three or ten or whatever, and/or those whose responses are awarded the most points by the judges. Results are posted on the Web site in a "Hall of Fame" and all players can see how well they did. E-mail games may also have prizes that are sent to the winner(s).

In a session entitled "Interactive On-line Learning: Using Games and Activities"[19] at the 2000 ASTD Conference in Dallas, Texas, Glenn Parker and Thiagi presented samples and examples of e-mail games. Many of these games are available free on Thiagi's Web site: www.Thiagi.com. In terms of the advantages of e-mail games, they listed "players being able to arrange their participation to suit their personal schedule" and "powerful any-time, any-place advantage at little or no cost" as key benefits of e-mail games. They also mentioned limitations such as the generous time deadlines necessary to meet the needs of global players sometimes leading to "players procrastinating and missing the deadline" and that players with "overflowing mailboxes may accidentally or intentionally ignore the e-mail notes about the game."

E-mail games are stand-alone training events that can serve as an effective training tool for a variety of purposes. They are inexpensive, relatively easy to design and deliver, and function in real time. They can take a fair amount of work to administer; but, if the subject matter is critical, the effort spent on such games can be well worth the investment with the payoff in ideas, group interactions, and group consensus.

Digital Game-Based Learning

Marc Prensky, the founder and CEO of games2train.com, uses the term digital game-based learning to describe the bringing together of learning theory and game technology in the creation of "games for adult learners that are used online or on computers."[20] Many of the learning games that have been created by games2train fall well within our category of electronic game-based training. Such games are the medium of delivery for learning content; they can stand alone as learning tools, be incorporated into a training program or, better yet, be used as a major force in a training initiative. These games are primarily content focused, but can also be experiential.

Prensky says his games are "designed to address a changing work force and bridge the chasm between the Boomer and Nintendo Generations."[21] Recent products from games2train, *Straight Shooter!* designed for Bankers Trust, and *The Monkey Wrench Conspiracy,* for think3 software, are described by Prensky as "the world's first fast-action videogame based training systems."[22] *Straight Shooter,* a 3-D videogame created for employee qualification and certification on any one of a number of topics, was designed for an employee population primarily under the age of thirty.

The Monkey Wrench Conspiracy, a Doom- and Quake-like videogame, complete with 'Agent Moldy,' is a tutorial that puts the player in the role of an intergalactic secret agent on a rescue mission. It is a complete tutorial for learning to use a complex 3-D design software program. The basic frame, that is, design and structure, of the game can be adapted and customized for other products and other industries. Such games can incorporate a social aspect by building a community around the game through the use of Web sites and e-mail.

For example, Prensky reports that *The Monkey Wrench Conspiracy* has become so popular that it has taken on a life of its own. Avid players now create new modules in response to new problems that are posted by other players.

Digital game-based learning can be done and done well, and it works. Prensky and other learning games providers have proven that. However, a major problem with such fast-action video game-based training systems is the cost—hundreds of thousands at the least, probably moving into a few million at the most. Right now, only major corporations facing drastic, company survival issues that require massive amounts of learning by global employees under the age of thirty are probably willing to invest such huge amounts. But things change. The costs will come down, the demand will expand, and digital game-based learning will emerge as a huge learning industry in the future.

Final Thoughts

The means are available to create more engaging e-learning through the use of interactive electronic games and activities. The question seems to be "what will it take to get designers to utilize the means?" The answer is most likely competition. The markets are so immense and the population of trainees under the age of forty is so huge that it is becoming imperative to attract and keep those learners. E-games are a good way to do just that.

It's sometimes difficult to imagine the future of e-learning. The paradigms of yesterday's learning keep getting in the way. In an article entitled "E-learning for the e-generation" Kevin Wheeler writes, "I doubt e-learning will ultimately look the way it does now. Today's e-learning is little more than a repackaged classroom. . . . Learning experiences [in the future] will be much more video-based and game-associated than we can even image."[23] Clark Quinn recently wrote an article called "mLearning: Mobile, Wireless, In-Your-Pocket Learning," which describes the future possibilities of e-learning through mobile computational devices such as palms, windows CE machines, even digital cell phones. He describes his vision further, "mLearning is the intersection of mobile computing and e-learning: accessible resources wherever you are, strong search capabilities, rich interaction, powerful support for effective learning, and performance-based assessment."[24] The possibilities are endless.

While e-learning may never completely replace classroom learning, it will be used more and more as a tool within classroom learning and within overall learning programs and initiatives. And, on its own, with infinite new electronic delivery modes and devices, the amount of electronic learning that will take place in the future is so great that it is unfathomable at this point in time.

The very nature of learning will change as well. In their *LiNE Zine Manifesto,* Brook Manville and Marica Conner write, "Learning is more important than ever. But in this New Economy, it's different than before. The new learning requires individuals and organizations to fundamentally change the way they talk about, work with, and act on what is known and what needs to be known in order to change, move, and grow."[25] Their challenging manifesto includes a future where the boundaries and identities between businesses and educational institutions blur, where e-learning will be only "one part of a rich mix of choice and mass personalized approaches to learning" and where the "distinction between formal and informal learning will and should evaporate."[26]

As a professional, your role as trainer or educator will undoubtedly shift, alter, transform, perhaps even mutate in the not too distant future, but games, electronic and nonelectronic, will still make an excellent medium for learning. And you will need to wisely choose and effectively use both traditional and electronic training games. Chapter 5 will give you practical, step-by-step guidelines for doing so.

In a Nutshell

E-learning is any training and education delivered, enabled, or mediated by electronic technology. This includes online learning, Web-based training, and computer-based training of all types. The training games that are part of e-learning can be assigned to the same categories as their nonelectronic counterparts: content-focused, experiential, or content and experiential frame games. Content-focused electronic training games are often electronic versions of paper-and-pencil games; whereas experiential e-games are either games that use electronic media to accomplish tasks for the purpose of experiencing the use of electronic media or variations of electronic simulation games. An electronic frame game is a generic electronic game template designed to be used with different types of content and that permits the instant design of new games. The most common are in the form of software for facilitator-led classroom electronic games or computer games to be incorporated into online training.

"Electronic game-based training" is another e-learning phenomenon in which the game can be the total medium of instruction. Two types of electronic game-based training are e-mail games and digital game-based learning. E-mail games are an inexpensive, content-focused form of training that is relatively easy to design and deliver, and function in real time.

On the other end of this continuum are expensive, fast-action videogame-based training systems that can stand alone as learning tools, be incorporated into a training program, or be used as a major force in a training initiative. These games are primarily content focused, but can also be experiential.

Notes

1. WR Hambrecht and Company (2000) "Overview: eLearning" <www.wrhambrecht.com>

2. Keith Gallagher, "A competitive business weapon," Random Thoughts column, *e-learning*, October 2000, p. 4.

3. Michael Moe, "E-learning in the New Economy," *e-learning*, July–August 2000, pp. 42–44.

4. Ibid.

5. Clark Quinn, "Engaging Learning," <http:itech1.coe.uga.edu/itforum/paper 18>, 1998.

6. Ibid.

7. Ibid

8. Patricia Galagan, "Helping members get up to e-speed" *ASTD*, July–August 2000, p. 56.

9. Brandon Hall, "The future of online learning," session M401, *ASTD* 2000 Conference, Dallas, Texas.

10. William Horton, <www.designingwbt.com>, 2000.

11. William Horton, *The Crime Scene Game*, <www.designingwbt.com>, 2000.

12. William Horton, *Games@Work presentation*, <www.horton.com>, 2000.

13. Owen Hall, (2000) *Simulation Showcase: E-sims*, NASAGA 2000 Conference, Minneapolis, MN.

14. Scott Fallows, *Simulation Showcase: E-sims*, NASAGA 2000 Conference, Minneapolis, MN.

15. Ibid.

16. *Gameshow Pro3*, <LearningWare.com>, 2000.

17. Ryan K. Ellis, "Software roundup: E-games" *ASTD Training and Development Journal*, August 2000, p. 72.

18. Thiagi Computer Game Shells, <www.thiagi.com>, 2000.

19. Glenn Parker and Thiagi, "Interactive on-line learning: Using games and activities," 2000 ASTD Conference, Dallas, Texas.

20. Marc Prensky, <games2train.com>, 2000.

21. Ibid.

22. Ibid.

23. Kevin Wheeler, "E-learning for the e-generation," *e-learning*, October 2000, p. 49.

24. Clark Quinn, *mLearning: Mobile, Wireless, In-Your-Pocket Learning*, <www.linezine.com>, 2000.

25. Brook Manville and Marcia Conner, *LiNE Zine Manifesto*, <www.linezine.com>, 2000.

26. Ibid.

PART TWO

THE PLAY'S THE THING

They questioned every item on the instructions. They manipulated the environment, bent the rules, tried to figure out "the real agenda," spied on other groups and were now taking apart the major equipment used in the game. I was grinding my teeth, checking my watch, and wondering why I deserved the training group from hell, when an image of Yoda came to mind. "Trust the process, Susan. Trust the process."

5

THE GAME KEEPER

CHOOSING AND USING TRAINING GAMES

Random House dictionary defines a game keeper as "the person in charge of the breeding and protection of game animals."[1] Once you begin using games in your training program, you will become a game keeper of sorts. You will choose and use your games with care. You will monitor and look after the games you use. You will protect your games from misuse and abuse. And, over time, you will develop new games and introduce them appropriately into the design of your training programs. Chapters 6 and 7 will cover designing and developing new games; in this chapter we will focus on assessing and selecting training games and effectively using those training games.

Training programs are designed and developed in numerous ways. Ideally, of course, they are designed and developed by qualified experts in response to discerning needs assessments and are designed to address the identified needs, in alignment with important company directives. Not so ideally, training courses are often put together hastily in response to some pressing need and may include a series of not so well-aligned activities and materials to accommodate the squeaky wheels of the moment. Most training programs fall somewhere in between.

Choosing the Right Game

If you are designing a new training program and would like to include a game in that program, you will want to spend some time considering how a game will fit into the overall design. The design document, or the program architecture, that is being developed is the "macrodesign," the big picture design. It answers the "big" questions. What is the purpose of this training program in its entirety? What are your key learning objectives? How long is the program? In what order will the concepts and materials be presented? As you look at the big picture of any training program, consider your key "learning moments" and the ebb and flow of energy throughout the training.

The "microdesign" of your program is a more detailed description of what will actually happen in the training to address each of your key learning objectives. The content, the learning activities, and the distribution of time for each of the learning objectives must be considered. Training games are one of many types of learning activities from which you can choose. There are various criteria that should be considered as you make your choices.

Michael Milano, with Diane Ullius, in his book, *Designing Powerful Training,* gives the following criteria to be considered when choosing a learning activity. "A good learning activity must:

- support the learning objective
- fit with the course content
- add variety to the course
- assist transfer of learning
- suit your participants
- conform to trainer competencies
- fit within logistical constraints

- work within time constraints

- be responsive to adult learners and learning styles"[2]

Shelia W. Furjanic and Laurie A. Trotman in their book, *Turning Training into Learning,* include additional criteria in selecting a game. A few of the questions they suggest you ask yourself when considering a game include: "Does the strategy for winning correspond with the learning objectives of the session? . . . If the game calls for using bells, buzzers, or other signaling devices, will these devices be accepted (or tolerated) by occupants of surrounding classrooms or offices? . . . Are all players allowed to actively participate?"[3]

A final question that Furjanic and Trotman put forth is, "Will the time invested in the game yield a worthwhile amount of learning?"[4] This is a question well worth considering. As mentioned earlier, it is easy to become infatuated with particular games. They can be irresistible sometimes—clever, fun, involving. But they can also be time consuming. If your program is limited in time and has a great deal of material to be covered, you will want to consider using games that do not take much time or games that cover a large amount of the material.

There are practical considerations also. I call these the trainer-friendly factors. If the training program is offered at different locations, you will want a game that is very portable. If you will literally be carrying the game to different locations, you will want it lightweight. If you will not have access to the training room in advance of the training, you will want a game that sets up quickly. Considering these types of factors in advance will help you in the long run.

If you already have a training program and you would like to add a game to that program, you still need to address the above procedures and criteria as much as possible. Stand back and think about your program. Review the design document and the purpose of the program. What are the key learning objectives? As you think about your important "learning moments" and the energy levels throughout the training, where is the best place for a game? What other learning activity will the game be replacing? Will it accomplish the same goal as the activity being replaced? Why are you considering the exchange of activities? What does the game add to the program?

You will also want to consider how many games and activities are too many. Training that is nothing but games and activities is not a good idea. Jumping from one game to another throughout a training session can become wearisome and give the appearance of lack of substance. This is especially true if the games and activities are not introduced well and are not explicitly tied into the learning objectives. Utilizing the debrief to reinforce the learning and the relevance of the game or activity to the real world is also important. Using games and activities that are smoothly integrated into the training can be very effective. It's the fluid integration that is key.

Right now, let's stop and consider for a moment, all of the factors that we have surveyed that make a training game truly effective, including those that constitute a good game, those that relate to course design, those that are based on theories of learning psychology, and those that reflect the trainer's needs and concerns. If we combined all of these elements into one list, and put that list into the form of an assessment, it would look like Figure 5.1.

Once you have decided on using a game, you will need to decide on the game. But first, consider what your "ideal game" would be like. Keeping in mind the criteria above, jot down your main requirements so that you can refer to them when you go big game hunting. Use the The Ultimate Training Game list. As you begin your search through the jungle of training games available to you, it is easy to get sidetracked and bedazzled by the vast displays you encounter. Beware the trainer who has become infatuated with a particular game and made the training fit the game rather than the other way around!

How Do You Find a Game?

Browse through libraries and bookstores. Go online and look around. Search through the catalogs, flyers, and mailers of companies who specialize in training materials. And the all-time preferred method: ask other trainers about their favorite games. As you peruse a variety of games, try to imagine these games being played within your program, with your participants, in your location, with you as facilitator. When you find a game that appeals to you and seems to be a good fit, see if you can observe its being used by someone else. If that's not possible, do a practice run of the game. Get a few friends and colleagues

The Ultimate Training Game Assessment Game assessed: Rate each item: 4 = excellent, 3 = good, 2 = fair, 1 = poor, 0 = awful					
Value as a Game:	4	3	2	1	0
1. fits with content, design, objectives					
2. is challenging and engaging					
3. adds variety and energy					
4. has objective, measurable results					
5. yields worthwhile amounts of learning					
6. has suitable strategy for winning					
7. works with various numbers of players					
8. has a high fun factor					
Learning Issues:					
9. repeats and reinforces key learning					
10. gives immediate feedback					
11. provides safe practice of new skills					
12. develops understanding of concepts					
13. provides meaningful challenge					
14. stimulates many senses					
15. promotes intense dialogue, discussion					
16. provides social contact, group work					
17. has realistic, complex experiences					
18. has analysis, interpretation, reflection					
Trainer Friendly:					
19. has minimal advance preparation					
20. fits time, space, and cost constraints					
21. fits trainer competencies					
22. is flexible and adaptable					
23. is nondisruptive to surroundings					
24. is easy to transport					
25. you like it!					
Comments: Add up your ratings and get a total score:					

FIGURE 5.1

together and try it out. See how they like it. Gather their comments and concerns.

If the game is part of a new program, you can try it and refine it during the developmental test and the pilot of the program. If you are using the game in a program that is already up and going, try it out in a session or two and see how it does. Even if you have to tweak it a little here and there, if it works well and meets your learning objectives, then you've got your game!

Before and After Playing a Training Game

Once you have chosen your game, there are a number of things that you can do to ensure using it most effectively. I'd like to share with you some of the basic guidelines for effectively using a training game that I personally have found helpful and that a variety of other trainers and educators recommend as well. I have considered calling this section "Susan's Lessons Learned the Hard Way," because so many of these guidelines are learned through experience. Hopefully, this information will save you some of the difficulties and mistakes that I plowed through at one time or another.

I'm going to share actions for you to take before and after the class or program in which you are using the game, as well as a three-step process to follow as you use the game. The last step in this three-step process is to conduct a debrief of the activity. This is certainly a very important step and the one written about the most in training literature. Let's begin with what to do before and after the class in regard to game playing.

Before Using a Training Game

The following guidelines are arranged in a suggested order as to when they should be done. Some you can do a few days before class; others need to be done right before training begins. There may also be a few items you will need to do during class right before the game begins.

Know Your Game.   The more comfortable and familiar you are with the game the better. If this will be the first time you have used the game in a class, practice using it beforehand. Practice with a group of real people if you can. Introduce the game just as you will in the class and then watch them play.

After they have played the game and you have debriefed it with them, ask them about the whole experience. Did they understand what they were supposed to do before they began doing it? If not, what could you have done differently in the introduction of the game? Was anything unclear as they played? What would have made the game go more smoothly? Be careful not to overanalyze and get too much critical feedback. You will find that you will get what you ask for, so be careful what you ask for!

If you can't have a real trial run of the game before the training event, at least have a full mental playing of the game. Literally, go through the introduction, playing, and debriefing of the game in your own mind, step-by-step. Imagine where you will conduct the game and how you will set it up. See yourself distributing materials and going over the purpose, the goal, and the rules. Imagine how the participants will go about playing the game. Play the game yourself and imagine different people going through the activity and doing whatever it is they will be doing. Play a full game using the materials and going through the entire process. Imagine problems that might occur and how you will handle them. Consider variations or changes you might need to make if things do not go as you expect them to.

Go through the debrief step-by-step in your mind. Consider a variety of ways that participants might respond to the debriefing questions. Imagine handling different issues that could be raised. Imagine a successful debrief and a pleasant ending to the entire game-playing experience.

Make Sure You Have All the Materials Needed.   If there are special handouts or materials that need to be printed or packaged in some particular way, do so ahead of time. Always have more than enough on hand. Don't count on getting something printed on the day before training! If there are things that can break, have a few extras on hand. If anything is battery operated, always carry extra batteries!

Put All Game Materials Together with a Materials List.   Put the game and all the materials needed for the game together in a box or carryall and keep it separate from your other training materials for that class. Don't mix game materials with other class materials. If the game has many different components and/or requires other special materials, for example, markers, sticky notes, paper clips, and so on, keep a list attached to the game box or your program folder and go through the list as you gather together your materials for the program.

Check Out the Game Playing Environment. It is always helpful, if possible, to take a look at the classroom or training space ahead of time. It is particularly important if you are using a game that has unusual or special space requirements. Look around the training space and decide where you will conduct the game and where the debrief will take place. If you cannot visit the actual site of the training until the day of the training, talk to someone on-site who can give you a good description of the training space and answer your questions. Then, get there early on the training day. If need be, you may have to do a little rearranging of furniture and you will want to have that completed before participants begin arriving.

You will not want the game-playing area to be the same area where you lecture. You will need enough training space to set up the game in a different area and enough room so that game players are not crowded. If the game is played in small groups, you will want some room between groups. You do not want players crowded or easily distracted by what's going on in other small groups.

All this said, however, it is best not to conduct the game in a separate room or in individual breakout rooms. You want to be able to easily monitor events. Participant learning that occurs in a game will feel more connected to the learning in other parts of the training program if the game occurs in the main room. Ask for a room that is large enough to conduct the game in the back, in a corner, or, if need be, temporarily rearrange the room in some way.

Prepare Any Necessary Group Instructional Materials. Consider how and where you will be introducing the game and giving instructions for how to play and how and where you will do the debrief. These should be two separate places, as will be discussed later. If you are using flip charts to introduce and debrief the game, write out the instructions and the key debriefing questions on the flip charts ahead of time. This can be done before you arrive and you can bring them with you, or do this as you are setting up the classroom well before participants begin to arrive.

Prepare the Classroom for the Game. A key decision to be made is where to play the game and where to debrief it. Once you have decided where you will be playing the game, do as much as possible to get that area ready for the game. You may be able to put key materials in that area ahead of time and even arrange furniture or props. At the very least, think through how you will ask participants to help you rearrange furniture and set up the learning environment when the time comes. Know ahead of time where you want to hold the debrief. It should be an area near, but slightly removed from the game-playing area, but preferably not back in the main lecture area. If you have any particular debriefing materials, put them in that area. And, if you have flip charts with debriefing questions or topics, post them on a wall near that area and cover them until the time you want to use them.

Prepare Yourself for the Game. Take a few moments to gather your thoughts about the game and to imagine its taking place. Stand in the space where you will be introducing the game and think about what you will be doing and how you will be doing it. Walk around the area, imagine the game taking place, and check for anything else that might need to be done. Consider the style in which you want to present the game: excited and enthusiastic? serious and mysterious? cool, calm and collected? Just take a moment to get a feel for the game and the game area.

After Using a Game

The following guidelines are arranged in chronological order. Some you can do immediately in the classroom after using a game, others need to be done right after class ends, and others after the class and before you use the game again.

Take a Short Break. When the entire game process is finished, the debriefing is complete, the moments of learning have occurred, and people are feeling good about the game, call for a short break. This allows the learning to sink in and a transition to be made to the next segment. It also allows you and the participants to move to another area of the training room, or put the room back as it was, and prepare for the next section of the training.

Gather the Parts of the Game.   As people stand and stretch and move about the classroom, you should immediately gather up the various parts of the game. You can certainly enlist the help of participants in doing this. If there are very large and cumbersome game components, you may want to leave these until the end of the class; but smaller pieces, parts, and components are best gathered sooner than later. If possible, put the game together as you will want it for the next time you use it. This will save you time later and cut back on parts and pieces lost! Put the game back into its box or the carryall and set it aside.

Prepare the Classroom for Continuing.   If the classroom was changed in some way for the game, put things back to the basic arrangement. If there were some products produced by the game, particularly something fun or positive, such as funny posters, clever summaries on flip charts, score sheets with team names, and so on, place these somewhere at the front of the classroom. These will serve as reminders of the game—the fun, the learning—and can be used for your closing summary.

Record Your Comments and Concerns.   This is something you should do throughout all of your training, but certainly in regard to playing games. Make notes to yourself during and after the game about different aspects of the game and how things went. Do this while the game is still fresh in your mind. Keep these notes some place that you can easily find when you are reviewing or preparing to do the training again: a folder with the game materials, or an outline of the game, or some place in your course materials. Note problems or rough spots and ideas for handling things differently. Keep a record of good illustrations and examples that occurred. You can use these in future playings of the game. Eventually, you can build a good supply of ideas, examples, stories, and improvements for using the game.

Don't Become Blasé.   Even the best of trainers can become a bit bored or blasé about a game that they use over and over. Get occasional feedback from a colleague about your performance in running a game. If you really want to shake yourself up a bit and work on your own performance improvement, videotape yourself running a game!

You may need to change the game or some aspect of the game in order to keep your own performance fresh and enthusiastic. When you find yourself "predicting" player responses before they are made, or "mimicking" participant answers in your head, take that as a warning sign and make some changes!

Playing a Training Game

The time has come to play a game. Three steps are involved in the playing of a training game: introducing or "setting up" the game, managing the game, and debriefing the game. Each step is important and the three steps build on one another. A game that is introduced and set up well will go much smoother and be easier to manage. A game that goes well and is managed well eases the way into an effective debrief. However, each step can also make up for mistakes or problems at an earlier step. So, ideally you'll want to do the best you can at each step; but if problems occur, and problems do occur, you can still have an effective game. In this section we will look into how to introduce and manage a training game; debriefing is a complex and significiant aspect of training games and will be covered in a separate section.

Introducing the Game
Your introduction to the game is very important. It's not just a time to tell people what they are going to be doing; it is an opportunity to aim the game in the right direction for a successful outcome. In the introduction, you want to set a positive tone, to motivate players to play, to alleviate fears and apprehensions, and to explain the game as clearly as possible. Sounds like a lot, doesn't it? It is.

Your Style.   Your attitude toward the game and game playing is crucial. Expectations affect outcomes. Your overwhelming belief in the learning benefits of the game should be very apparent. Experts suggest that if you are positive and enthusiastic, the participants will respond accordingly. So, put some energy and enthusiasm into your introduction.[5] Your expectations for a positive, interesting, high participation event will help make it happen.

Tell the group that they are now going to play a game and ask them to stand, stretch, and move with you into the game-playing area. As you do this, change your basic demeanor. Put forth more energy; increase your pace and volume; use broader gestures; smile! "Speak with clarity and authority."[6]

The Set-up.   Begin to motivate people to play the game by using both rational and emotional appeals. Rationally, explain the overall purpose of the game, the "why they are playing this game." Establish the relevance of the game to the content of the course. For instance say, "This game we are about to play will give you a chance to practice much of what we have been talking about this morning. It will help you recognize when and how to use the key behaviors."

This is also a good time to address reluctance and safety issues. For example, "Now, we've all agreed that these six key behaviors that we've been discussing this morning are critical to your success as new managers. This game will give you the opportunity to practice those six key behaviors in a safe and secure environment, and have a good time doing so."

You might want to motivate them further by sharing examples from past sessions in which people have both learned and even enjoyed learning by using the game. For example, "The class last month was a little reluctant to play at first and then I couldn't get them to stop. In fact, after class, Barbara Hendrix borrowed the game to use with her people over at the 14th Street office; and it took me forever to get it back!"

The Instructions.   Once you have set the stage for the playing of the game, the next step is to give the purpose of the game and go through the instructions. It is helpful to have these listed on a poster or flip chart in the game-playing area. You can use them as you present the purpose and instructions and the players can refer to them during the game.

Stand in front of the visual display of the purpose and instructions; and, as you go through, point to the item you are discussing. This reinforces what you are saying and establishes the display for future reference. Experts in the field suggest you begin with the purpose of the game.[7] State it simply and directly: "We are playing this game to further develop your coaching skills."

Next, explain how to play the game using a step-by-step approach. Try to keep this as simple as possible. If there are more than half a dozen steps and more than a few basic rules, you may want to consider using a game handout so that players can easily refer to their own copy of instructions whenever necessary.

The basics that you need to cover in the instructions include the following:

Type of Game and Overall Theme of the Game
Tell the players what type of game they will be playing and give them some idea of the theme or the context of the game. For example, it might be a futuristic board game or a game of Bingo with a diversity theme.

Roles and Responsibilities
Let players know who they are in the game and the basics of what they are supposed to do. Describe the persona they are to take on and their major task in the game; for example, "You are time travelers moving around the game board trying to get from the year 2010 to the year 2025," or "You are individual players asking other players to sign your Bingo card."

If you notice that someone is having difficulty with the idea of playing the game, see if you can ascertain their concerns and address those concerns. Occasionally someone may ask not to play. Agree to their request and assign them a role in managing or monitoring the game in some way. Ask them to be an observer and take notes on what they see happening. Or for some games, you might ask them to be a scorekeeper or the timekeeper. But do find some way to keep them involved with the game playing. Do not excuse anyone from participating.

Objective and What Is a Win
Players want to know the main objective or goal of the game and what they have to do to win. Give them this information in an enthusiastic manner: "In order to win, each player on your team must get to the year 2025 and the team must have a combined score of 100 points. Let's see if every player and every team can win before 3:30!" Or something like this: "Your goal is to reach midnight without losing all of

your time, energy, and sanity points. When we get to midnight, I will call an end to the game and the teams can count the cards they have left. The team with the most points wins the game."

Where and How They Play

Let participants know exactly where they will be playing the game. Point out and/or demonstrate where and how they will play. For example, if they were playing a card game or a board game, you might walk over to one of the tables and say, "You will be playing in groups of four at these game tables." Picking up a sign from that table, you continue, "Each table has a sign with the names of the four players who will be playing at that table. A little later when I say 'go,' you will proceed to your assigned tables and begin your games."

Resources and Time

Let players know what different resources they have and how much time they have to play the game. Hold up examples of playing materials; show them game pieces, playing boards, card decks, and any props. Indicate where or how they can obtain additional materials as needed. Give them an estimate of how long the game will take to play; or, if there is a time limit, tell them what it is. For instance, if they are playing a board game and you are standing next to a game table, as you would say the following, you would hold up examples: "Each team will have a game board, a stack of Anticipation Cards, and a pair of dice. Each player will have a token to move around the board. What you want to do is have each player on your team move his or her token to the finish square by 3:30. That means you have 45 minutes to play the game."

Rules and Regulations

The rules of a game guide the action and put limits on behavior.[8] You will need to go through the rules, explaining and giving examples, such as the following: "Rule number three says, 'You may not communicate by speaking during the game.' This includes speaking in any language, even sign language. However, you may use gestures and sounds to communicate."

Instructor's Role

Let the players know what you will be doing during the game. In most games you will have a very passive role. Let them know this. Announce that you are not a player and that once the game begins, you will step back and let them be responsible for their own game playing. Once the game begins, you will want to locate yourself away from the action, but in a spot where you can see what's happening. If something goes wrong, call a "time-out" and fix the problem, or go over the rules again if needed. Then allow the game to proceed and go back to your observation spot.

What Ends the Game

Players need clear instructions about what ends the game. They will want to know how to tell when the game is over. Be very explicit and demonstrate. You should say something like, "When your 30 minutes is up, I will blow this whistle [blow the whistle] and that will indicate that the game is over. When you hear the whistle, stop where you are and count the number of cards you have left."

Special Concerns

Jeff Stibbard, in his book *Training Games—from the Inside,* suggests, "Any special concerns or problems with the game should be mentioned in the directions."[9] This includes things like physical safety, noise levels, keeping everyone involved, being polite, respecting property, and so on. For example, you may want to point out possible safety issues involving equipment, such as "Please be careful when you enter the carpet and don't trip on these cords." Or you may state concerns for noise levels with, "I know how exciting it gets at the end of this game, but let's not get too carried away with noise making. There is a class next door!"

Dividing into Groups

If you need to divide a class into small groups to play a game, how many should there be in each group? Now that's a good question. The answer, of course, is, "That depends." And it does depend on at least three factors: What kind of a game is it? How much time do you have? How "personal" is the game?

Board games and card games, unless stated otherwise in the directions, work best with small groups of three to five players. Acting and artistic games work better with slightly larger groups of five to eight players. Simulation games tend to take eight or more people and may require the entire class in one game. More physically interactive games, especially those held outdoors, often work better with groups of eight to twenty. None of this is cut and dried, of course; and games that you buy should have directions that discuss the number of players that work best. If you are designing your own games, you can follow these general group-size suggestions and then adapt as needed.

In general, the more people playing a game, the longer it will take. Getting six tokens around a game board takes longer than getting three around, and so on and so forth. If a game involves players giving personal information or discussing difficult or sensitive topics, a smaller group size will feel safer and also make it harder to withdraw and not participate. In a diversity training class I teach, I use the *Diversity Deck*[10] cards for a discussion game in the afternoon. I initially put the participants into three groups of six to eight people, but after a session or two, I tried small groups of three or four players and found the level of energy and participation was much greater. The discussion cards present examples of workplace situations reflecting diversity issues; and the players have to discuss what the problem is, why it's a problem, and what should be done about it. I think the sensitive nature of the discussion cards made people reluctant to speak up and really discuss the issues in the larger group. For some reason, the smaller group of three or four people did just the opposite.

Another thing to be aware of when dividing the class into groups for game playing is player personalities. A good mix is helpful. You don't want all the quiet, shy people in one group and all the talkative, dominating types in another. It also helps to mix players from different departments, functions, locations, levels, and so on.

There are many ways to divide participants into smaller groups. They can number off, say one through six, and then all people who are number ones form a small group, as do all people who are number three, and so forth. You can write group names or numbers on small pieces of paper, fold them and put them in a paper cup. Each participant can then draw a paper for his or her assigned group. For some games, you may want to deliberately mix the groups in some way; this you can do by writing out the names of participants and their assigned groups on a flip chart paper or an overhead transparency.

Do Not Pre-empt the Learning!

This point is stressed by Leigh and Kinder in their book, *Learning Through Fun and Games*.[11] It's a significant point, but is sometimes difficult to achieve. Some games have surprise events, interesting twists and turns that occur during the game, that lead to major learning points. You don't want to give away too much information about these events and spoil the learning, but you don't want to sound unsure of yourself when presenting instructions and answering questions. It helps to have some type of response ready when a participant asks a question that you don't want to answer. You can say something like, "I really don't want to answer that question. It's better to go ahead and play the game and not worry about that." Then quickly move on.

I have found that there is usually a very analytical, problem-solving participant who immediately starts trying to "figure out" the game. I will sometimes jokingly state, "All right now. I can see those wheels churning in your head, trying to 'figure out' the game. I'm sure you can do so, but I'm going to ask that you just play the game and enjoy it and you can use your 'figuring out skills' after the game to help me with the debrief. OK?" This usually works pretty well. I have acknowledged their behavior and their ability and asked for their help. Most people will respond well to this.

Managing the Game

There are three basic behaviors involved in managing a game: starting the game, monitoring the game, and ending the game.

Start the Game.   Once you have introduced the game, gone through the instructions and rules for playing, you ask them to start playing. You may want to be a little dramatic in doing this. Pause a moment, hold your hands up in the air, and with authority ask, "Is everybody ready? OK. Play the game!" Then step back and away.

Monitor the Game. As was stated earlier, in most games you will have a very passive role. Once the game begins, find a comfortable place for yourself away from the action, but in a spot where you can monitor what's happening. You may want to take notes, but downplay or minimize this if you do. You do not want participants feeling like you are judging them or evaluating their performance. On the other hand, you do want to observe how players play: Are they focused? Is there confusion? Is there any ineffective or disruptive behavior? You can weave your observations into the debrief after the game.

You may also take on what Jeff Stibbard calls "an overseeing role," that is, keeping score, watching the time, and taking notes.[12] Or, you may want to assign these duties to participants when you set up the game. My own experience has been that it is sometimes better to assign these roles to the group if there are enough participants to cover such duties and still have active participation in the game, or if there are people who can't play for some reason. But the nature of the game and the learning situation should also be considered. There may be times when it is more effective for you to do some of these tasks, particularly if they are not complicated or intrusive.

If something goes wrong during the game, you can call a "time-out" and fix the problem, or go over the rules again if needed. Then allow the game to proceed and go back to your observation spot. I remember once when we were using the Interel electronic carpet maze for a team-building game, two engineers playing the game decided to take apart two tables in the training room and build a bridge across the carpet. One of them immediately found a screwdriver and they started turning over a table. Fortunately, the tables did not come apart easily and I was able to call a time-out before their mission was accomplished. I had to ask the players not to use furniture or any other items or equipment from the classroom to help them get across the carpet. Every time we make use of the carpet maze now, I add a rule about not employing any other items to help them get across the carpet. I have also been giving the "table deconstruction story" as a humorous example for that rule.

End the Game. When the time is up and/or the game is over, stand and move into the game-playing area and announce, "time's up" or "stop" or blow a whistle, ring a bell, play the chimes, or clap your hands. Whatever you have agreed upon as the signal for the game to end. Wait for everyone to stop what they are doing and silence to fall over the group. Then say, "Thank you" and tell them where and how you want to conduct the debrief.

Debriefing the Game

Much has been written about debriefing interactive learning events and for very good reasons. There is much to be said and debriefing is critical to establishing and reinforcing the learning. Unfortunately, this is also the point in the game-playing process where the less skillful trainer may try to "save time" in the program by cutting it short and moving on to the next item on the day's agenda. Don't do it!

Ken Jones explains "In its military origin debriefing was a form of intelligence gathering" and suggests that the debriefing begin with establishing the facts and with letting participants "get things off their chests."[13]

Jeff Stibbard calls the debrief "the sting in the tail, . . . where the real learning takes place."[14] He recommends moving physically and mentally into the debrief and says this can be accomplished by doing the debrief in an area separate from the game-playing area, but not the "sitting and listening" area of the classroom. Just a slight move to the back, or the side, of the game-playing area would work. Asking participants to get chairs and form a circle in or near the game-playing area is a good technique. Even asking participants to remain standing in the game area, but perhaps forming a circle or a semicircle would be helpful. However, do be aware of the fact that many participants become physically uncomfortable if they have to stand for very long. So if you expect the debrief to go beyond fifteen minutes or so, it is best to have the participants seated.

When participants have arranged themselves, tell them you will give them a moment to collect their thoughts and then do so. As they sit or stand quietly for a moment or two, you can clear your own mind and get into a "debriefing mode." The debrief does not necessarily have to take a long time. It should provide enough time for a full review of and reflection upon the major dynamics of the game. In general, experiential games are more likely to involve emotional events and reactions, and therefore, include more "aha's" in the debrief. And this may take more time.

Because some debriefing sessions can take a fair amount of time, it is important to keep the discussions to the point and moving along, but not hurried. Try to emphasize meaning and application of the learning more than just a repeating of what happened. If you noticed certain unproductive behaviors being used during the game and they are not mentioned by the participants in the debrief, be sure to insert a question or two in the debrief that addresses these behaviors and have participants discuss them. If the game took a fair amount of time and participants are in need of a break, it is best to take the break first and debrief afterwards.

What to Cover in a Debrief

In regard to what should be covered in the debrief, the old training maxim, "what, so what, and now what" is a pretty good guideline. An effective debrief should review what happened in the game, then discuss the significance of those happenings, and finally, have participants plan for the application of what was learned. Different authorities suggest different categories of debriefing questions, but 'what, so what, and now what' are always covered in some form or another.

Leigh and Kinder, who see the trainer's role in a debrief as being "to guide the conversation and draw out the quiet members,"[15] suggest a sequence of three basic questions: "What happened? How do you feel? and What are real life parallels?"[16]

Stibbard suggests that after creating a debriefing environment, you give your own quick overview of what happened, and then take participants through guided questions.[17] Thiagi recommends six key debriefing questions: How do you feel? What happened? What did you learn? How does this relate? What next? What if?[18]

I suggest a debriefing procedure similar to all of these. For short content-focused games, you might choose to cover only four areas: What happened? What did you learn? How does this relate? Where do you go from here? However, if the game was fairly long and touched on important issues, you will want to include: How do you feel? For experiential games and content-specific games that contained emotional events and reactions, you will definitely want to include "How do you feel?" either to begin the debrief or right after "What happened?"

If you know the game very well and the major points you want to cover, you might choose to list only the four or five key questions on a flip chart page. For longer, more complicated debriefs, you will want to list key points under each major debriefing question. You can put each focus question at the top of a separate flip chart page and under each, put a few bullet points related to that particular game. For example:

1. What Happened?
   - How did you begin?
   - Roles and responsibilities
   - Easy vs. difficult
   - Any conflict?

2. How Do You Feel?
   - Positives? Negatives?
   - Frustrations, disappointments
   - Satisfactions, successes
   - Other reactions

3. What Did You Learn?
   - What worked? What didn't?
   - Cooperation, competition
   - Communication issues
   - Any "do differentlies?"

4. How Does This Relate?
   - To your job?
   - Your department?
   - Your company?
   - To our training purpose?

5. Where Do You Go from Here?

- Applications?

- Further information?

- Comments, questions, concerns?

When Things Go Wrong

The effective use of training games also involves an awareness of the potential problems that can occur when playing games, and the ability to deal with those problems. Such problems can originate from a variety of sources including the participants, the environment, the game, the trainer, and endless variations and combinations thereof. Let's take a look at some of the problems you might encounter and some strategies for dealing with them.

The Participants

In training with games, as in all other training circumstances, there will always be participants who may need "special handling." If you have *quiet, shy or more introverted participants,* you may need to draw them into the activity with direct questions or by asking them to comment on another participant's remarks. If you have a number of quiet participants who are not participating as fully as you would like, you can include short dyad and triad discussions throughout the debrief. For example, you might say, "Everyone get a partner please. Now, take a minute or two and discuss with your partner what you learned from this game." After a couple of minutes, you can ask the partners to report back to the whole group.

The partner technique also works with *participants who talk too much.* I have found that after a minute or two, it helps to say something like, "OK, you still have another minute or so. Don't forget to have both people share their thoughts!" You can also use the technique of going around the group and one-by-one letting people give their thoughts or observations. There will be times when an incessant talker just keeps talking regardless of the technique being used. At these times you may simply have to interrupt the person, thank them for their sharing, and call on someone else. Sometimes it may feel awkward doing this, but other participants will appreciate your doing so.

There are times when you will have *a very negative participant* who, for whatever reasons, will complain and criticize the game playing. A little of this is all right, and as the game unfolds, such participants will often change their tune. However, if the negative person is being disruptive or having a dampening effect on the group, you will want to deal with the behavior immediately. A good technique is to turn to the group and get their opinions on what the person is saying. For example, "Brian has just voiced his concern about this game's being a waste of time. How do the rest of you feel about this?" The majority of the participants should jump in here and support the game playing. If they do not, then this may indicate that the game was not set up as well as it should have been. You may need to reestablish the value of the game by using your own credibility with the group or giving them additional information.

You will sometimes have *super competitive participants* who become so involved in "winning" that they make it difficult for other participants to enjoy and learn. This may indicate a need for some tweaking of the game to make it less likely to bring out this type of behavior. If you wait, group members will often handle this type of behavior themselves; and you can always direct the debriefing to discuss it. If it really gets out of control and begins to cause extreme problems, you can always stop the play for a moment, comment on the behavior and ask for a change in behavior and then begin the play again.

Occasionaly *players will revolt* and change the rules or change some major aspect of the game. If the changes don't affect the learning outcomes, leave them alone, let them play and discuss the changes in the debrief. Such behavior can provide particularly good learning points in the debrief. If the changes in the rules or procedures are dangerous to the safety of the players or may damage the property in some way, or if they will completely ruin the learning experience and have a major damaging effect on the program, call a "time-out" and modify the changes.

When you have *participants with special needs,* you may have to adapt the game in some way to accommodate those needs. Always be aware that some participants may have difficulty with vision and hearing, so talk loud and clear and occasionally move among the participants as you speak. You should also have the major instructions for the game posted on flip charts in fairly large print. For games requiring physical movement, you can give participants who are not mobile a monitoring role such as keeping score, watching the time, or observing for certain behaviors.

It is also important that trainers be aware of *cultural differences among the participants.* Certainly when training abroad or training groups with large numbers of participants from other countries or different cultural backgrounds, the trainer must check the games and game material for anything that might be considered offensive or very strange. This is particularly true of experiential games that involve physical contact and physical closeness. If you find yourself in such a situation and have time in advance, you may want to check with friends and colleagues who have knowledge of the cultures in question. Or if there is no time, check with the participants themselves.

For example, you could say something like, "At this point in our program, I am considering our playing a game. However, this game involves our standing in a circle and holding hands. I know that in some cultures this might not seem appropriate and since we have two or three different cultures represented here, I thought it might be helpful to talk about how such an activity would be perceived in different cultures." Then go on to have such a discussion and make your decision regarding the game according to what you learn in the discussion. Needless to say, you should always have a backup game or two ready if needed.

The Environment

The environment can have an impact on how successful the game is. If there is not enough space in the classroom, you will want to check before the class to see if you can find another space to use for playing and debriefing the game. If what seemed like an appropriate space before the game began, turns out to be a problem in some way once the game gets started, you may have to stop the game, make adjustments, and then continue.

If the game becomes very loud and starts disrupting learning in nearby classrooms, interrupt the game and ask the players to quiet down a bit. If the classroom is visible to others and a crowd begins to form to watch the game, you may have to monitor the crowd or even turn them away if their observing gets in the way of the learning!

The Game

Sometimes, for whatever reason, *the game doesn't work!* Nobody wins. They can't solve the problem. They get stuck somewhere in the process and go no further. You give them an extra five minutes and still the game doesn't work! When the time is up, stop the game and debrief. Say something like, "Usually when I use this game, the group solves the maze and gets across the carpet in fifteen or twenty minutes. This time, even with the extra five minutes, no one has gotten through the maze and across the carpet. Time is up. Let's form a circle with some chairs in the back corner and debrief what's happened."

Keep your tone up-beat and/or neutral. Don't get upset or discombobulated because "it didn't work." Do not emphasize the fact that "the game didn't work" or that "they couldn't solve the puzzle." Don't intercede and try to fix things. Just accept what has happened and focus on the learning. Trust the learning process. Trust the game and the course design. I have seen some incredible "aha's" occur in debriefs following "games that didn't work!"

Sometimes if you are using a popular learning game that is available on the market, there will be *participants who have played the game before.* If there are only one or two people, you can use them in monitoring roles or perhaps they can agree to play again but not to "give away" key information. If you find over time that more and more participants have played the game, you will need to find a different game, or at least, a backup game to use when needed. When you have a backup game, in the introduction to the training, check to see how many participants have played the game and whether you will need to use your backup game. That way you can begin to make whatever logistical changes are necessary early in the training and not get stuck with a sudden need to change things!

The Trainer

There are a number of trainer behaviors that can interfere with the effectiveness of a training game. For example, trainers must be careful *not to give too much information* about a game ahead of time and decrease some of the game's impact. Nor should a trainer set *unrealistic expectations* by giving a game a lot of hype ahead of time. It is always better to undersell and over-deliver a training game.

In their book *More Games Trainers Play,* Scannell and Newstrom make the following observation, "Insecure, inexperienced, or unprepared trainers may *use games to kill time,* to impress upon trainees *how smart they are,* or to *put down trainees.* When playing the games begins to dominate the focus of the learning process, most trainees will perceive the games as being fake or cute, but distracting from the overall professionalism of the program."[19] Always remember to connect the game playing with the goals of the training during your introduction and again in the debrief.

Final Thoughts

The care and concern of the trainer who facilitates a training game can have a tremendous impact on the effectiveness of the game and the power of the learning. Just as it is with effective training, the combination of a skillful trainer and a well-designed training mechanism—be it program, activity, game, or whatever—is the best possible combination. We have all experienced the variety of combinations: a terrific trainer saddled with mediocre material, an excellent training game mangled by an unskilled trainer, and, of course, the worst combination of all—the truly awful material made unbelievably worse by a tedious trainer.

Your goal in using training games should be to attain the best possible combination of effective training game and skillful delivery of that game. When you carefully chose a training game, you are helping that combination to occur. When you take the time and effort to deliver a training game in the best manner possible, you are further ensuring that best possible combination. The same time and effort will be required in designing effective training games, as we will see in the next two chapters.

In a Nutshell

There are many factors to consider in choosing a training game: the placement of the game within the design of the training program, the qualities of the game itself, the learning aspects of the game, and the factors related to the trainer's abilities, needs, and concerns. All of these factors are not only helpful in choosing a game, but are also useful in assessing a game that you are already using.

Once you have an effective training game, getting the most out of that game by skillfully using the game is your next concern. Simple preparations before and after the game, and following basic guidelines for introducing, managing, and debriefing the training game can help you reinforce learning and utilize your training game to its fullest. All of this information is not only critical for choosing, using, and assessing training games, but it is also quite valuable when you begin designing your own training games as you will see in the next chapter.

An assessment (Figure 5.2) and two checklists are given at the end of this chapter. I developed the assessment using the factors from The Ultimate Training Game list and will be using it in the next chapter as we look at designing training games. The factors that we have looked at in regard to what to do before and after a training game are presented in checklist form at the end of the chapter, as are the basics to cover in game instructions.

Charts and Checklists

The Ultimate Training Game Assessment
Game assessed:

Rate each item: 4 = excellent, 3 = good, 2 = fair, 1 = poor, 0 = awful

Value as a Game:	4	3	2	1	0
1. fits with content, design, objectives					
2. is challenging and engaging					
3. adds variety and energy					
4. has objective, measurable results					
5. yields worthwhile amounts of learning					
6. has suitable strategy for winning					
7. works with various numbers of players					
8. has a high fun factor					
Learning Issues:					
9. repeats and reinforces key learning					
10. gives immediate feedback					
11. provides safe practice of new skills					
12. develops understanding of concepts					
13. provides meaningful challenge					
14. stimulates many senses					
15. promotes intense dialogue, discussion					
16. provides social contact, group work					
17. has realistic, complex experiences					
18. has analysis, interpretation, reflection					
Trainer Friendly:					
19. has minimal advance preparation					
20. fits time, space and cost constraints					
21. fits trainer competencies					
22. is flexible and adaptable					
23. is nondisruptive to surroundings					
24. is easy to transport					
25. you like it!					
Comments: Add up your ratings and get a total score:					

Before and After Playing a Game Checklist

Before:

- Know your game
- Make sure you have all the materials needed
- Put all game materials together with a materials list
- Check out the game playing environment
- Prepare any necessary group instructional materials
- Prepare the classroom for the game
- Prepare yourself for the game

After:

- Take a short break
- Gather the parts of the game
- Prepare the classroom for continuing
- Record your comments and concerns
- Don't become blasé

Basics to Cover in Game Instructions

- Type of game and overall theme of the game
- Role and responsibilities
- Objective and what is a win
- Where and how they play
- Resources and time
- Rules and regulations
- Instructor's role
- What ends the game
- Special concerns

Notes

1. *Random House Dictionary* (New York: Random House, Inc., 1988).

2. Michael Milano with Diane Ullius, *Designing Powerful Training* (San Francisco, CA: Jossey-Bass/Pfeiffer, 1998).

3. Shelia Furjanic and Laurie Trotman, *Turning Training into Learning,* (New York: American Management Association, 2000).

4. Ibid.

5. Jeff Stibbard, *Training Games—from the Inside* (Australia: Business & Professional Publishing Pty Limited, 1998).

6. Joe E. Heimlich, "Constructing Group Learning,"*Learning in Groups: Exploring Fundamental Principle, New Uses and Emerging Opportunities,* no. 71, edited by Susan Imel (San Francisco, CA: Jossey-Bass Publishers, 1996).

7. Elyssebeth Leigh and Jeff Kinder, *Learning through Fun and Games,* (Australia: McGraw Hill, 1999).

8. Ibid.

9. Jeff Stibbard, *Training Games.*

10. Susan El-Shamy and Gayle Stuebe, *The Diversity Deck: Situations Reflecting Diversity Issues* (Bloomington, IN: Action Pack Learning Card Series, Advancement Strategies, Inc., 1993).

11. Elyssebeth Leigh and Jeff Kinder, *Learning through Fun and Games.*

12. Jeff Stibbard, *Training Games.*

13. Ken Jones, *Interactive Learning Events: A Guide for Facilitators,* (London: Kogan Page, 1988). (Distributed in the U.S. by Stylus Publishing.)

14. Jeff Stibbard, *Training Games.*

15. Elyssebeth Leigh and Jeff Kinder, *Learning through Fun and Games.*

16. Ibid.

17. Jeff Stibbard, *Training Games*.

18. Sivasailam Thiagarajan (Thiagi), "How to Design and Guide Debriefing" *The 1999 Annual: vol. 1, Training* (San Francisco, CA: Jossey-Bass/Pfeiffer, 1999).

19. John Newstrom and Edward Scannel, *More Games Trainers Play* (New York: McGraw-Hill, 1983).

At 6:00 A.M. on an already humid August morning in the Heartland Hotel in Mount Pleasant, Iowa, I suddenly woke up and realized that I had forgotten to bring the major component of the opening game for my Applied Creativity class. I sprang from bed, frantically got dressed, jumped in my car, and headed for the twenty-four-hour grocery store across from the manufacturing plant where class would begin at 7:30. Stalking the aisles with my imagination struggling to get out of first gear, I stopped in front of the "sewing and crafts" display. For $1.25 each, I grabbed ten long, clear plastic, quilting sticks. At 7:40 A.M. I was introducing the rules of the game, "You have exactly fifteen minutes to find a use for the object; name the object; and write a slogan for the object." Whew, that was a close one.

6

LET THE GAMES BEGIN

EXAMPLES AND ILLUSTRATIONS

Let's move a little further down the road of training games into the realm of designing training games. Even if you are an experienced trainer, wise in the ways of training with games, or someone new to the use of games in the classroom, the time will come when you will want to add a training game to a training program and cannot find an existing game to meet your needs. As you approach the realm of game design, let the same criteria that directed your selection of a training game direct your design as well. Go to the Ultimate Training Game Assessment (Figure 6.1) and let those criteria guide the development of your training game.

The Ultimate Training Game Assessment
Game assessed:

Rate each item: 4 = excellent, 3 = good, 2 = fair, 1 = poor, 0 = awful

Value as a Game:	4	3	2	1	0
1. fits with content, design, objectives					
2. is challenging and engaging					
3. adds variety and energy					
4. has objective, measurable results					
5. yields worthwhile amounts of learning					
6. has suitable strategy for winning					
7. works with various numbers of players					
8. has a high fun factor					
Learning Issues:					
9. repeats and reinforces key learning					
10. gives immediate feedback					
11. provides safe practice of new skills					
12. develops understanding of concepts					
13. provides meaningful challenge					
14. stimulates many senses					
15. promotes intense dialogue, discussion					
16. provides social contact, group work					
17. has realistic, complex experiences					
18. has analysis, interpretation, reflection					
Trainer Friendly:					
19. has minimal advance preparation					
20. fits time, space, and cost constraints					
21. fits trainer competencies					
22. is flexible and adaptable					
23. is nondisruptive to surroundings					
24. is easy to transport					
25. you like it!					

Comments: Add up your ratings and get a total score:

FIGURE 6.1

Games appear in training for a variety of reasons and to solve a variety of problems. Here are five situations in which you might decide to design a training game; maybe some of them will sound familiar.

Situation 1. You might decide to use a game to solve a particular problem in the design or implementation of an established program.

Situation 2. You might have an activity within a program that needs energizing and decide to make it into a game.

Situation 3. Maybe you will be designing a new training event and want to use a game to meet a key learning objective.

Situation 4. Perhaps you will be concerned about prework for a program and decide to use a game to get it done.

Situation 5. Or, just maybe, you'll be considering a training topic, mulling over ideas in your mind, and suddenly the idea for a game will pop into your head!

All of these situations have happened to me and I chose to design a training game to deal with each of them. However, these are only five situations; needless to say, there are many others. In this chapter, I will take you through each of these five situations and how a training game was developed. Think of this as "a behind the scenes look at why and how these games were designed" and how they are presently being used in training programs. For each example, I'll give you:

1. an introduction, a short history, and a description of the game
2. instructions on what to do before and after the game, how to introduce and manage the game, and how to debrief the game
3. an assessment of the game using the Ultimate Training Game Assessment
4. some final thoughts and observations about the game

All trainers have different individual styles and all training games can be used in a variety of effective ways. Most of these games I have used many times and I am sharing the way that I've learned to utilize them; your own style and use of them could be quite different. In fact, you will find that you may change the way you use a game depending on the group you are working with and the objectives you are teaching towards.

Let's begin with a simple word search game, and then move on to a card game, a board game, an e-mail game, and an experiential activity game. As you read the descriptions about introducing, managing, and debriefing the games, see if you can visualize the classroom and what is taking place. See if you can imagine yourself using the training game.

Situation 1. A Problem in Program Design
Introduction
I was teaching a very straightforward, standard feedback program to supervisors in a large factory and was having trouble getting the program off to a positive start. This was one of those mandated training classes in which participants come dragging in late and sit as far in the back as possible. The people who had designed the course had evidently not had my type of audience in mind. The opening exercise was a discussion to define effective feedback and elicit the characteristics of such feedback from the group. My carefully phrased, open-ended questions would usually get met with blank stares and long periods of silence, somewhat reminiscent of the high school discussion scenes from the movie, *Ferris Bueller's Day Off*.

I tried making lists of characteristics—some good, some bad, some ugly—and having participants go through the lists choosing the ones that they thought would describe effective feedback. That helped a bit. But when I brought in a Word Search on Effective Feedback and made a game of it, prizes and all, I actually got participants to participate.

I put together this word search in two or three hours, tested it, refined it, and used it. It gets people doing something immediately and it gets them thinking about feedback. This game is not published anywhere; and, if you would like to make use of it, please do.

This word search is a content-focused paper-and-pencil game that can be used to identify gaps or weaknesses in knowledge about effective feedback and to stimulate discussion. It's a fun, nonthreatening way to get participants energized and discussing the characteristics of effective feedback. It can also be used as part of the summarizing at the end of a course. A good way to handle the prizes for this type of game is to have a bowl of wrapped candies that you pass around for winners to take one. With the class I just described, I found it was better to walk around the room with the bowl, letting winners take a piece of candy. Can you guess why?

Game 1: Word Search for Effective Feedback

Objective: To review some of the characteristics of effective feedback and elicit a discussion of those characteristics.

Summary: Participants are given a word search handout and have ten minutes to find as many descriptors of effective feedback as they can. They then discuss the characteristics they have found and others they think should be added to the list. A final round of play is used to find descriptors of ineffective feedback.

Time: About 30 minutes.

Number of Players: Any number can play.

Equipment: One copy of the word search (Figure 6.2) for each participant, or each pair or group of participants.

Before and After Playing This Game

There is very little to do before this type of game. Familiarize yourself with the answers and make sure you have enough copies of the game. You might want to make overhead transparencies of the word search: one with no markings, one with the positive characteristics marked, and a final one with the ineffective characteristics marked. After the game, it helps to quickly make note somewhere of additional characteristics that came up in the discussion. These may be useful for later classes.

Introducing the Game

Take an upbeat fun approach to the game. As you walk around the group and distribute the game sheets face down in front of people, talk about this being "a quick warm-up exercise to get everyone thinking about feedback." Ask them to keep the papers turned down until you say to turn them over. As you continue distributing the papers, ask how many of them know how to do word searches. See if you have anyone

D	E	V	I	T	C	E	J	B	O	G
A	E	L	A	T	E	S	L	A	F	A
F	E	S	A	G	C	S	M	O	P	R
A	S	I	C	T	U	E	P	P	Z	E
B	I	N	G	R	E	E	R	U	V	L
R	C	C	N	K	I	O	O	I	F	E
I	N	E	O	S	P	P	T	H	D	V
E	O	R	L	R	S	E	T	C	C	A
F	C	E	I	X	T	D	I	I	T	N
M	E	A	N	A	E	R	M	S	V	T
W	T	Y	V	S	A	B	E	H	K	E
E	O	I	A	E	C	N	L	U	D	E
Q	R	I	L	U	O	F	Y	X	R	N
P	B	C	S	H	O	R	T	W	O	T

FIGURE 6.2

in class that does a lot of word searches. If so, ask that person to explain how most word searches work.

As the person explains, you finish distributing the papers and go to the front of the class. Thank that person, and reinforce or repeat the basics of what they have said. Tell the participants that this is a word search game about effective feedback. Explain that they will have ten minutes to find as many words as they can that describe effective feedback. There are fourteen words and they might be found across, or down, or diagonally. They can run forwards or backwards.

You might say, "I'll let you know when the ten minutes are up; then, everyone stop and count how many words you have found. There are fourteen words. Anyone who finds all fourteen words wins a prize." (This is always a good time to bring out the bowl of candy.)

Managing the Game

When everyone is ready to play, look at your watch and say, "Ready, set, go!" Stand to the side of the room and let people play. When there are two minutes left, you might say so. Let them know when time is up and ask them to count how many words they found.

Ask how many people found all fourteen, then how many found thirteen, and twelve, and so on. Have them get a partner and share and compare the words they have found. Two's can form groups of four and so forth until they are all able to find all of the words. Let them give you the words they have found. List them on a flip chart or white board. If there are some they can't find, show them where the words are on the overhead of the word search. Pass out the prizes to the winners.

Get a discussion going about these characteristics and ask for other descriptors that participants feel should be added to the list. Discuss these other characteristics as they come up and add them to the list as the group directs. Try to reach group consensus regarding the final list. When the list seems complete to both you and the participants, ask which characteristics are most important and why. See if the group can agree on a rank ordering of the final characteristics. Then, offer a two minute bonus round to find the six characteristics of *ineffective* feedback and give additional prizes to those who find all six in the two minutes.

Debriefing the Game

Your debrief of this game does not have to be long, but don't skip it. You want to reinforce the fact that they have learned something from playing the game and that what they have learned is important. You might want to have the debriefing questions on an overhead or printed on a flip chart. Ask how they feel. Ask what they learned.

If anything comes up during the game that you want to make sure gets included in the debrief, add it to the flip chart while they are playing the game, or make a note of it during the discussion and add it to the flip chart during the debrief. You can use something like the following printed on a flip chart:

- What happened?
- How do you feel?
- What did you learn?
- How will you use what you learned?

Assessing This Game

Using the Ultimate Training Game Assessment and the criteria that we established in Chapter 5, I would assess this game as shown in Figure 6.3.

Final Comments

As you can see from the assessment, in and of itself, this game is above average, but not exceptional. However, within the program it can serve to stimulate the learners and involve them with the subject matter and that's important! A skillful trainer can take this above average game and use it to reinforce key learning concepts regarding effective feedback. It can be used to get the learners thinking about feedback and what is important regarding the giving and receiving of feedback and it can do so in a nonthreatening, fun manner. This can help pave the way into further learning about feedback.

There are various ways to modifiy this game. If no one finds all fourteen, then those with the highest number win. If there are a lot of people who are not familiar with word searches, or if the participants do not know each other and you want them to interact a bit, you can

The Ultimate Training Game Assessment
Game assessed: Effective Feed-back Word Search

Rate each item: 4 = excellent, 3 = good, 2 = fair, 1 = poor, 0 = awful

Value as a Game:	4	3	2	1	0
1. fits with content, design, objectives		✓			
2. is challenging and engaging		✓			
3. adds variety and energy		✓			
4. has objective, measurable results		✓			
5. yields worthwhile amounts of learning		✓			
6. has suitable strategy for winning		✓			
7. works with various numbers of players	✓				
8. has a high fun factor			✓		
Learning Issues:					
9. repeats and reinforces key learning		✓			
10. gives immediate feedback		✓			
11. provides safe practice of new skills			✓		
12. develops understanding of concepts		✓			
13. provides meaningful challenge			✓		
14. stimulates many senses		✓			
15. promotes intense dialogue, discussion		✓			
16. provides social contact, group work		✓			
17. has realistic, complex experiences				✓	
18. has analysis, interpretation, reflection		✓			
Trainer Friendly:					
19. has minimal advance preparation	✓				
20. fits time, space, and cost constraints	✓				
21. fits trainer competencies	✓				
22. is flexible and adaptable	✓				
23. is nondisruptive to surroundings	✓				
24. is easy to transport	✓				
25. you like it!			✓		
Comments: Add up your ratings and get a total score:	77				

FIGURE 6.3

have them play this game with partners or in small groups of three or four people. The two parts to this word search—the positive characteristics and the negative ones—can be played at different times. You can hold a discussion on effective characteristics after the first part and then move on to a discussion of ineffective characteristics and surprise them with a final word search for the six ineffective characteristics.

Word searches are easy and fun to make on your own, but if you haven't got the time or the knack to do so, take a look at the puzzlemaker section on *DiscoverySchool.com*.[1] They have a great word search design program for educational use only. Once you have a word search or a similar word puzzle, just add some structure, make it a competition with prizes and you've got a short, energizing game.

Situation 2. An Activity Needs Energizing

Introduction

My partner, Gayle Stuebe, and I were developing a number of card games and activities for team development to accompany a deck of learning cards that we had designed. I was using the cards in a team-building program with newly formed departments within a large toy manufacturing company. This group was a trainer's ideal group—bright, motivated, and very involved in the training.

This card game began as a discussion activity in which a deck of *Cards for Developing Teams*[2] was being used to elicit the ideas and opinions of team members in regard to what they could do to become more effective and efficient. By doing this discussion activity, participants would hopefully better understand the relationships among these team characteristics; the characteristics would become more real; and team members would reach a better understanding of how the characteristics were reflected in their own team. In order to encourage people to be both more critical and specific in this exercise, I had added the instruction to "choose the ten that you feel are most important for your team," and it did make the exercise much more dynamic. However, it also made for much longer discussions that were already taking a lot of time because the team was so large. I learned that team members tend to become very serious about this activity and sometimes go on and on in their discussions.

So, I made an on-the-spot decision to break the team into three groups. I took a very positive, upbeat approach to the change in directions and asked each group to move their table to a different corner of the room. I gave each small group a deck of cards and asked them to choose their top ten most important characteristics of an effective team and list them on a flip chart. I gave them time limits, said that there would be prizes for levels of agreement among the teams, checked my watch and said, "Go!" While they worked away, I went to the cafeteria and bought some small bags of cookies for prizes and then came back to watch their discussions.

Making it into a game with time limits and prizes and taking an upbeat approach, really helped energize the activity and move things along. The act of splitting up the team, having them do something and then coming together to compare their views worked so well that I have since used this approach with smaller teams as well.

When I noticed that the top ten characteristics that were being chosen by the three groups were not the same, I interjected the requirement to rank order their top ten on the flip charts and gave them ten extra minutes. They then shared and compared their ratings and finally reached agreement as to which ten they would all choose. Prizes were given to the group that had the highest number of the final top ten characteristics on their individual top ten list. Since the prize was bags of cookies, and this was a team-building course, the prize was shared among the whole team and everyone took a break.

After the break, I had the team rate themselves on their top ten characteristics and this led into action planning for how to improve in the areas where they scored lowest. There is some good information that surfaces when the team is split and then brought together to compare results. Very similar results indicate a consensus of what characteristics are important and dissimilar results indicate the opposite. The trainer can use this information to move and motivate the team toward improvement and action planning.

The game finally evolved into a game called The Top Ten, which appears in *Card Games for Developing Teams*.

Game 2: *The Top Ten*

Objective: To have team members consider what team characteristics are important to them and how well they are reflecting those characteristics.

Summary: Team members discuss the fifty-two team behavioral characteristic cards and then choose the ten they feel are most important. These are rank ordered and then used to assess the team.

Time: 60 to 90 minutes.

Number of Players: Any number of team members.

Equipment: One copy of the *Cards for Developing Teams* and a flip chart with markers for every group, plus a flip chart and markers for the facilitator. Prizes that are appropriate for a group.

Before and After Playing This Game

There is not much preparation for playing this game. It helps to be very familiar with the *Cards for Developing Teams*. You will want to prepare debriefing flip chart pages ahead of time and have them nearby and ready for the debrief.

If this is a team of twelve or more members, it works better to divide them into two groups as I described earlier. In fact, this has become my favorite way of playing this game even with a smaller team. The additional energy it provides can be helpful particularly if you have a very serious group.

After playing the game, make a copy of the ten characteristics they choose and how they assess themselves in terms of each. Put this in your files for that group. It can be very useful in further training that you do with them.

Introducing the Game

There is a fine line between getting the group interested in playing a card game and raising false expectations about what they will be doing. You want to get them attentive and ready to engage in the activity, but you don't want them to start visualizing Las Vegas card tables. So, let them know right away that they will be playing a card game, but not the usual type of card game that they may be used to. Tell about the card deck, how it is constructed of fifty-two cards each with a characteristic of effective teams described on it. Explain the four sections of thirteen cards each: unity, communication, support, and performance. If the group has not used decks of learning cards before, pass around the deck and let them look through the cards.

Say that the purpose of the game is to have them consider the characteristics of an effective team and which characteristics are most important to them. Explain that the game has three parts—discussion, rank ordering, and assessing—and that they will be playing in two groups. Write the purpose, "Decide on the top ten characteristics of an effective team" at the top of a flip chart with bullet points underneath that say:

- Discuss all fifty-two characteristics
- Choose your top ten
- Rank order your top ten
- Assess your team

Then gather up the deck that they have been looking through, divide the team into two groups by having them number off A-B-A-B around the room. Put the A's at one table and the B's at another and give each a *Cards for Developing Teams* deck. It helps to have the groups pick group leaders for the activity; it can be particularly helpful with larger groups. Ask the group leaders to open up the decks, take out the cards, shuffle them, and put them in the center of the table. Explain how this discussion activity works and that they will have only forty minutes to do it, which is not a lot of time. Tell the group leaders that they will have to keep the activity moving along and that you will let them know when they have ten minutes of discussion time left.

Managing the Game

Since this game is played in three parts, you will have to stop them at each segment, give directions for the next segment, and then let them continue. As you monitor the game, look for people getting sidetracked into long discussions that are not helpful. Again, it is sometimes difficult to decide just how much discussion should take place. You want them to really consider the characteristics and discuss what they mean and how important they are, but you don't want them to get bogged down in semantics or minutiae. If you notice one group or the other taking too much time, interrupt the activity and say something like, "I know it's easy to get sidetracked into in-depth discussions, but try not to. Keep the discussion moving quickly. You now have about twenty minutes left to discuss the rest of the cards. So, if you have not gotten half way through the deck by now, try going a bit faster."

Let me say at this point, that if you have the time and the discussions seem very beneficial, it is quite all right to extend the time allotted for this activity. If that happens, just interrupt for a moment and say that they are doing so well with the discussions that you've decided to give them some additional time. Tell them how much and say again that you will let them know when they have ten minutes left.

I have found it helpful to speed up the introduction to the second segment of this game. Tell them that for this segment, they will have ten minutes in which to choose what they think are the ten most important characteristics of a team and to rank order them from the most important to the least important on their flip chart. It also helps to tell them at this point that a good way to establish the top ten and rank order them is to lay the chosen cards out on the table and move them around. Tell them that if they can choose their top ten and get them rank ordered on their flip chart in ten minutes, they will get a prize! Then look at your watch, wait a few seconds and say, "Go!"

You may want to give them a one- or two-minute warning. When the ten minutes are up, stop the activities and give prizes to the group(s) who have listed ten characteristics on their flip charts. For this type of activity try giving prizes that can be shared such as a large bag of popcorn, a bowl of grapes, a package of cookies, or pencils with humorous designs or slogans. Teacher supply stores have great collections of pencils for awards!

As you hand out the prizes, say that there are still two more tasks for them to complete. First, you want the two groups to combine and then decide on their final Top Ten Most Important Characteristics as a whole team and then write this out on a separate flip chart page. If they accomplish this in five minutes or less, they will all get a prize! Give them five minutes, and if and when they accomplish this task, give them a prize they can all share.

For the final task, ask them to assess themselves as a team on each of the ten characteristics using a scale of 5 to 0 with 5 = excellent, 4 = very good, 3 = good, 2 = fair, 1 = poor, and 0 = awful. When they finish this, compliment them on their hard work and their accomplishments and say that you would like to debrief the activity. You may want to have a short break before the debrief.

Debriefing the Game

The debriefing of a game like this can be very beneficial to the team. Your purpose is to let the learning sink in and to reinforce it. If possible, move the group to a new setting. Or, if they are at different tables, ask them to join the tables and pull their chairs around the new, larger table. As they do this, you can pull over your flip chart and get your pre-prepared debriefing sheets ready. Ask them to take a moment and think about the training game and what they learned. Wait a couple of minutes, then turn over the first page of your debriefing flip chart pages and begin.

1. How Do You Feel?
   - About the game? about the team?
   - Frustrations, disappointments?
   - Satisfactions, successes?
   - Other reactions?
2. What Happened?
   - How did you begin?
   - Roles and responsibilities
   - Easy vs. difficult
   - Any conflict?
3. What Did You Learn?
   - Which characteristics were immediately chosen by all groups?
   - Which were ranked highest, lowest?

- What did you learn about yourselves as a team?
- Cooperation - competition?
- Communication issues?
- What else?

4. How Does This Relate?
   - To your job? your team? your workplace?
   - Your department? your company?
   - To our training purpose?

5. Where Do You Go from Here?
   - Applications?
   - Further information?
   - Comments, questions, concerns?

Assessing This Game

Using the Ultimate Training Game Assessment and the criteria that we established in Chapter 5, I would assess this game as shown in Figure 6.4.

Final Comments

This type of card game can be very flexible in regard to time. It can be done quickly in forty to sixty minutes or done in a very thorough, in-depth manner for up to two hours or more, depending on the group and the purpose and objectives of the program. You can even do the first game components, discussing all characteristics and then choosing and ranking ten characteristics, early in the course, and wait and do the assessment of the team later. Doing so adds a feeling of connectedness to the content.

Situation 3. Design a Game to Meet a Learning Objective

Introduction

This content-focused board game with a futuristic outer space theme was designed specifically to have participants practice a three-step model for anticipation that is central to an Advancement Strategies

The Ultimate Training Game Assessment
Game assessed: Top Ten Card Game

Rate each item: 4 = excellent, 3 = good, 2 = fair, 1 = poor, 0 = awful

Value as a Game:	4	3	2	1	0
1. fits with content, design, objectives	✓				
2. is challenging and engaging		✓			
3. adds variety and energy		✓			
4. has objective, measurable results	✓				
5. yields worthwhile amounts of learning	✓				
6. has suitable strategy for winning			✓		
7. works with various numbers of players	✓				
8. has a high fun factor			✓		
Learning Issues:					
9. repeats and reinforces key learning	✓				
10. gives immediate feedback		✓			
11. provides safe practice of new skills		✓			
12. develops understanding of concepts	✓				
13. provides meaningful challenge		✓			
14. stimulates many senses	✓				
15. promotes intense dialogue, discussion	✓				
16. provides social contact, group work	✓				
17. has realistic, complex experiences			✓		
18. has analysis, interpretation, reflection	✓				
Trainer Friendly:					
19. has minimal advance preparation	✓				
20. fits time, space, and cost constraints	✓				
21. fits trainer competencies	✓				
22. is flexible and adaptable	✓				
23. is nondisruptive to surroundings	✓				
24. is easy to transport	✓				
25. you like it!		✓			
Comments: Add up your ratings and get a total score:	**88**				

FIGURE 6.4

course on anticipation skills. The first half of the course has a great deal of information and interesting discussion activities, but I felt that the actual ability to use the model, to apply the model in a natural, almost spontaneous manner, could not be achieved unless participants had a great deal of practice in doing so. I wanted an interesting, nonthreatening activity that would give small groups of participants the opportunity to apply the model repeatedly, but did not want to bore them in the process. I felt that a board game was a good way to accomplish this.

Originally, players recorded the events, consequences, and actions that they generated in the game on pages in their class workbooks. This was a little awkward because they would have to have their workbooks with them around the game board. I also found that there were times when I wanted to use the game in short training sessions or as part of presentations I would make on anticipation, and it became more useful to have separate game booklets that I could use anytime I wanted to play the game. So, we now use small booklets along with the game and they work very well.

Game 3: Future Flash

Objective: To practice using a three-step Effective Anticipation Model and write down as many things as possible to do now to be better prepared for the future.

Summary: Players roll dice, move pawns around a game board, draw cards, and read about future possible events. These events are discussed and all players record possible consequences that such events might have and any actions that they might take now to be better prepared for such future possible events. Play continues until all players at each game board arrive at the year 2020. The first player at each game board to arrive at 2020 wins a prize.

Time: Each player's turn should take three to five minutes. The entire game usually takes about sixty minutes.

Number of Players: Any number can play with two to four players per game board.

Equipment: Enough game boards for all participants to play; one die, one set of Event Cards, one set of Chance cards, and four pawns for each game board; one game booklet for each player.

Before and After Playing the Game

The day before using this training game, make sure you have all the materials that you need. If the game is in a box, open it and check to make sure everything is there. I speak from experience; there is nothing worse than opening the game box to get the game set up during a break in the training, and finding important materials missing. Running down the hall to find a copying machine or desperately writing complex instructions on a whiteboard minutes before the game begins, is not what you want to be doing minutes before the game begins!

The event cards in this game need to be checked now and then to make sure they are still only "possibilities" and have not yet occurred in the real world. Occasionally new cards will have to be developed and added to the game. After the game is over, put the pawns, die, and card decks back into their separate plastic bags and put the plastic bags and game boards together in a separate box. If you do this immediately and carefully, you won't have to redo it later.

For this game, decide early in the training where and how you will have them play the game. If the classroom is arranged with tables in a U-shape, pull extra chairs to the inside of the U and group players two on one side and two on the other, then leave some space, and put another two on one side and two on the other, and so on around the U-table. If there are two rows of tables arranged in U-shape, have the front row turn and play in sets of four with people in the back row. If there are small round tables, you can have one game per table. For larger round tables, it becomes more difficult and you may want to set up extra tables in the room for the game.

Think ahead of time about how you will divide the participants into game-playing groups. If there are people you do not want playing the game together and/or people you want to mix and match for whatever reasons, make the groupings ahead of time and write them out on an overhead transparency or on a flip chart. When the time comes, you can show the group divisions and assign each grouping to a table or playing site. If separate tables are being used for the game, put tent cards with numbers or letters on the tables and give each grouping on your list a table number or letter.

Also, think about the debriefing of the game and how you want to conduct it. Prepare some flip chart pages with key debriefing questions and have them ready a few pages back in the pad of flip chart paper or ready to hang on a wall in the debriefing area. Or, you could have the debriefing questions on an overhead transparency to use when the time comes.

Introducing the Game

Tell the group to get ready for a trip to the future; they will now be playing a board game called Future Flash! Reveal the groupings and ask players to stand and stretch and go to their assigned tables. If rearranging chairs is needed, enlist the help of participants and get them all involved in preparing their environment for the game.

When people have settled into their new arrangements, distribute the game booklets and go over the purpose and basic structure of the game. Distribute the game boards and the plastic bags of pawns, dice, and card decks. Ask them to take out the pawns and decide who will use which ones. Then have them take a look at the two card decks. Then ask them to look at the game directions in their game booklets and follow along as you go through them.

Go through the directions, then read an example Event Card and have the group help you generate possible consequences and actions to take now. If they have trouble with this, take them through another example or two. If people have trouble generating actions to take now, explain that sometimes the only actions that can be taken now are to keep informed about what's happening.

Emphasize that the first person at each game board to reach the year 2020 is the winner and will receive a prize. Say that since different groups will finish at different times, you want the remaining players to keep playing until all groups have had at least one winner. The early winners can help by participating in the discussions of those still playing. Offer a grand prize to the game group with the most winners.

Managing the Game

There is not much managing to be done with this game. An occasional question may come up regarding the content of a card, or what to do if you keep landing on Chance spaces, but there is usually little for the instructor to do during this game. In fact, if you are an extrovert like I am, you will have to be careful not to start hanging around the games, adding your comments to every discussion!

Award prizes to each first winner in each game group when they get to 2020. Make the prizes something that can be easily shared. After each game group has a winner, you should stop the game. Ask the participants to stay in their game board groups for one more task. Say that you will give them ten minutes to look through all of the events, consequences, and actions to take now that they have listed in their booklets and come up with three trends that they see in the near future and three actions to take for each trend. Tell them there will be prizes for each group that completes this assignment. Look at your watch, pause, say, "go," and let them work.

When time is up, say "stop," and have them stop and share their results. You can create a flip chart page with a listing of the various trends and actions that they generate and use these for other course activities, especially action planning. Pass around a bowl of candy and have winners, which most probably will be everyone, take some candy. Ask them to pause for a moment or two and think about the game and what they learned.

Debriefing the Game

If the players are at tables in a separate part of the room, move a flip chart back into that area and list their trends and actions to take on that flip chart. Then, hold the debrief in that area of the room. If they are at various arrangements around the classroom tables, move a flip chart to an area where they can all see you and have them stay where they are for the debrief. Ask them to move their chairs a bit so that they can see the flip chart and then take a moment or two to think about the game and what they learned. This will help move them mentally from a playing mode into a debriefing mode.

Use basic debriefing questions with any additional questions you like, such as the following:

1. How Do You Feel?

   • About the game? about the future?

   • Frustrations, successes?

   • Other reactions?

2. What Happened?
  - How did you begin?
  - Strategies, techniques?
  - Easy vs. difficult

3. What Did You Learn?
  - About yourself and the future?
  - The possible, probable and preferable?
  - What else?

4. How Does This Relate?
  - To your life, your future?
  - To your job? your workplace?
  - Your department? your company?
  - To our training purpose?

5. Where Do You Go from Here?
  - Applications?
  - Further information?
  - Comments, questions, concerns?

Assessing This Game

Using the Ultimate Training Game Assessment and the criteria that we established in Chapter 5, I would assess this game as shown in Figure 6.5.

Final Comments

One issue that has come up with this game is the problem of keeping it current. With the constant increase in technological advances and scientific breakthroughs of the past few years, I find that an almost constant updating of the event cards is necessary. When I designed this game nine years ago, I would check the cards every year and take out a few event cards that had recently become reality and add a few new cards. Now, I find that it's necessary to check the cards every few months and add and subtract as needed. This is not too difficult since I make new cards from a form I have on my computer. I pull up the card

The Ultimate Training Game Assessment
Game assessed: Future Flash Board Game

Rate each item: 4 = excellent, 3 = good, 2 = fair, 1 = poor, 0 = awful

Value as a Game:	4	3	2	1	0
1. fits with content, design, objectives	✓				
2. is challenging and engaging	✓				
3. adds variety and energy		✓			
4. has objective, measurable results	✓				
5. yields worthwhile amounts of learning	✓				
6. has suitable strategy for winning	✓				
7. works with various numbers of players	✓				
8. has a high fun factor		✓			
Learning Issues:					
9. repeats and reinforces key learning	✓				
10. gives immediate feedback		✓			
11. provides safe practice of new skills	✓				
12. develops understanding of concepts	✓				
13. provides meaningful challenge		✓			
14. stimulates many senses	✓				
15. promotes intense dialogue, discussion	✓				
16. provides social contact, group work	✓				
17. has realistic, complex experiences			✓		
18. has analysis, interpretation, reflection		✓			
Trainer Friendly:					
19. has minimal advance preparation		✓			
20. fits time, space, and cost constraints	✓				
21. fits trainer competencies	✓				
22. is flexible and adaptable		✓			
23. is nondisruptive to surroundings	✓				
24. is easy to transport	✓				
25. you like it!	✓				
Comments: Add up your ratings and get a total score:	**89**				

FIGURE 6.5

form, put in new content, print it, and cut the cards. Then I add the new cards to the decks and take out any that have moved from possibilities into actualities. So far, the time and effort required to keep these decks current is well worth the value the game brings to the training.

Situation 4. Getting Prework Done Before a Class

Introduction

While writing this chapter, I decided that it would be nice to have an "e-mail game" example. However, I have not designed or used an e-mail game as part of any class that I have taught yet. But the idea of doing so was intriguing. As I thought about the different types of training situations where e-mail games might be helpful, I remembered a leadership institute that I facilitated for a number of years and the difficulties we had in getting the participants to do prework for the five-day course.

Five days is a long time and it is often difficult for people to take that amount of time away from their jobs; therefore, the thought of doing class work before they arrive at the institute is anything but appealing! This particular institute had people from different parts of an international corporation coming together to look at the "bigger picture," to discuss common issues and challenges, and to network and expand their connections in the corporation. Getting familiar ahead of time with some of the issues and material to be covered during the week can be very helpful, but very difficult to accomplish. The idea of using an e-mail game to get people discussing and thinking about some of the course material prior to arrival seemed perfect! It would also be a way to get participants acquainted ahead of time and looking forward to more time together. So, this game idea is new and has not been tested, but it has great potential. I will describe it here and if you would like to use this game idea, please do!

In the past, participants in the program received packets in the mail containing articles to be read and forms to be filled out. Over time, the basic registration materials and information forms had all been changed to e-mail delivery back and forth. What I think would be extremely helpful and time saving would be to have an institute Web site that would contain general information and logistics about the institute, and all of the basic course materials, background reading assignments, and any other course information—all easily accessible. The Web site could also serve as the "home base" for prework e-mail games.

Prework e-mail games could be designed around basic issues or questions related to the training objectives. Institute participants could receive e-mail game materials inviting them to brainstorm ideas around at least one, or maybe a number of questions. All ideas would then be listed on the Web site. Participants could then vote for the best ideas and predict the ideas that they think will rank in the top ten. This could go on for two or three rounds prior to the institute, with the final fourth round occuring just a few days before their arrival at the training event. Final winners could be announced and introduced at some point during the first day.

Game 4: E-mail Brainstorming

Objective: To have institute participants become familiar with and thinking about basic issues before the institute begins and to introduce institute participants to one another prior to the program.

Summary: Institute participants receive e-mail game materials inviting them to brainstorm ideas around at least one of three basic issues. All ideas are listed on the Web site; and participants vote for the best ideas. Participants predict what they think will be chosen as the top ten ideas. Winners are those who most closely predict the outcomes, those whose ideas are ranked among the top three or five or ten. Results are posted on the Web site in a "Hall of Fame" and all players can see how well they are doing as the game continues. Final announcements of winners and "Hall of Fame" top ranking players and so forth are announced during the first day of the insitute.

Time: The four rounds are begun three weeks prior to the program and are completed on the first day of the program.

Number of Players: More than twenty, but not more than fifty. Twenty to thirty is most managable.

Equipment: Access to e-mail and the institute Web site.

Before and After Playing This Game

If there is a Web Site for the program or the department sponsoring the program, that should be the Web site used for this e-mail game. If that is not possible, then you will have to have access to a Web site that can be used for the game. The easiest way to prepare for the game is to have the instructions located on the Web site along with the location where the ideas submitted by the players will be listed. You will also put your "Hall of Fame" listings at this location.

Before this game you will have to very carefully write out the instructions and steps to be taken for the game. Maybe do a test run to make sure everything works and check on the amounts of time needed for each step. If there are a number of international participants, you may have to give more time for each round. If you use more than one topic or issue, you will want to make it clear in your introductory materials that players can choose one or more topics to work on.

State each of the issues or problems in a "how to" or "ways to" format. For example, "how to implement new processes more quickly" or "creative, quick ways to get new hires up to speed." For each issue, create categories or subdivisions for the ideas that will be generated. This will make it easier to deal with the ideas when they begin pouring in. Give examples and illustrations whenever possible so that players know exactly what is expected of them. Explain how you will handle similar ideas. Maybe list all ideas under the various categories and indicate which were determined as "new" ideas when they arrived.

There are two parts to the play: collecting ideas and then voting for ideas. You may want to set up a specific number of ideas as a goal for the players to reach and end the solicitation of ideas when that number is reached. A hundred and one ideas is a common goal that is used. You might want to go for the top two hundred or use a number that has some significance to the organization. You can also use a cutoff date and time and not accept additional ideas after that time and date. The point here is to keep the number of ideas that you receive to a manageable number! You will also have to decide on a scoring system and put that information into the overall game information. You can give one point per new idea listed or maybe use ten points per new idea to inflate scores a bit. (I always prefer receiving eighty points to eight points, don't you?)

You can also add an element of judging to the game by having a panel of judges give extra points in some way. Perhaps to the best over-all idea, the top ten ideas, the player submitting the most ideas, the company location submitting the most ideas, and so on and so forth. Any extra element of fun or competition adds to the effectiveness of the game.

Once the set number of ideas has been reached, the second part of the game, the voting for the best ideas, begins. Ask each player to review all of the ideas listed and vote for the ten top ideas. Create a spreadsheet and record the votes as they come in. Save the results for announcement at the first day of the program. You can select the players whose ideas were voted among the top ten, or if you want fewer winners, the top five. You can also have special awards for the players with the most ideas, the craziest ideas, and so on.

An e-mail training game like this will entail a fair amount of work for the facilitator—before, during, and after the game. After the game, you will want to review the steps and procedures and do whatever you can to streamline them for the next time the game is played. If you do this well for the first time or two you play the game, your job will be much easier for future games!

Introducing the Game

Your tone and approach to introducing and setting up this game should be done with the audience in mind. You may want to take a challenging, somewhat competitive approach or go for the creative, fun, out-of-the-box approach. Since this type of game may be very new to many of the players, explain the relevance of the issues, the richness of the ideas that can come from this type of activity, and then make the instructions as clear and straightforward as possible. It wouldn't hurt to put a little hype into the fact that "winners will be announced at the institute."

Tell the players what issues they can choose from and give them an example or two of types of ideas. Explain that the game is played in rounds, that the rounds have time limits for ideas being submitted, and that the final round is a voting by all players for the top ten ideas.

Managing the Game

When players start sending in their ideas, the ideas need to be saved in a particular location. Let players know that you have received their ideas by sending them an e-mail "thank you" and telling them to check the Web site for the list of the results. You will need to list ideas as they arrive. At the end of the time set for the first round, you will need to give points for each new tip (it's new if it hasn't been submitted by anyone else up to the point that you receive it). Create a spreadsheet of players' names, rounds, and bonus events, and then enter the points received at the end of each round. At the end of each round you can identify the players who have the ten highest scores and maybe send out an e-mail to all players announcing the ten leading scorers at that point and directing players to check the Hall of Fame.

Keep updating the lists of ideas and sending out e-mails announcing the beginning and end of the various rounds. As players begin to respond and take part in the game, it will be important to incorporate and post their ideas as quickly and accurately as possible. Take the game through round three (or however long it takes to collect your set amount of ideas) and the beginning of the last round where players vote on the best ideas, but save the identifying of final winners for announcement in the class.

Debriefing the Game

The debriefing of this game will happen in the classroom and should follow the usually topics of a debrief: what, so what, now what. If players of this game have not used e-mail games before or were skeptical about the game, be sure to include a "feelings" debriefing topic. Also, be sure to include discussion of the use of the game to get players curious about one another. Debriefing questions could be something like the following:

1. How Do You Feel?
   - About the game? about e-mail?
   - Frustrations, disappointments?
   - Satisfactions, successes?
   - Other reactions?

2. What Happened?
   - How did you begin?
   - What was easy? difficult?
   - What kept your interest?
3. What Did You Learn?
   - Which ideas surfaced immediately?
   - Which were most unusual? helpful?
   - What did you learn about yourselves?
   - What did you learn about each other?
   - What else?
4. How Does This Relate?
   - To your job? your workplace?
   - Your department? your company?
   - To our training purpose this week?
5. Where Do You Go from Here?

Assessing This Game

Using the Ultimate Training Game Assessment and the criteria that we established in Chapter 5, I would assess this game as shown in Figure 6.6.

Final Comments

This type of game can take a lot of work the first few times you do it, but once the method is understood and a procedure has been developed, it requires much less time. To really snag and keep the interest of your participants, you must make the issues and questions extremely relevant and meaningful to them. These must be issues that they struggle with daily and are in great need of ideas to address. You might also want to increase the credibility of the game and its helpfulness by involving a special guest or even a mystery guest or two. Well-respected or admired executives, local experts, or even a celebrity of sorts might work well in this role. Your own dedication to the quality and efficiency of this type of game will pay off in the achieving of top-notch ideas that will be valued and used by the participants.

The Ultimate Training Game Assessment
Game assessed: E-mail Brainstorming

Rate each item: 4 = excellent, 3 = good, 2 = fair, 1 = poor, 0 = awful

Value as a Game:	4	3	2	1	0
1. fits with content, design, objectives	✓				
2. is challenging and engaging		✓			
3. adds variety and energy	✓				
4. has objective, measurable results	✓				
5. yields worthwhile amounts of learning		✓			
6. has suitable strategy for winning	✓				
7. works with various numbers of players	✓				
8. has a high fun factor			✓		
Learning Issues:					
9. repeats and reinforces key learning		✓			
10. gives immediate feedback		✓			
11. provides safe practice of new skills			✓		
12. develops understanding of concepts		✓			
13. provides meaningful challenge			✓		
14. stimulates many senses			✓		
15. promotes intense dialogue, discussion		✓			
16. provides social contact, group work			✓		
17. has realistic, complex experiences				✓	
18. has analysis, interpretation, reflection		✓			
Trainer Friendly:					
19. has minimal advance preparation		✓			
20. fits time, space, and cost constraints	✓				
21. fits trainer competencies		✓			
22. is flexible and adaptable		✓			
23. is nondisruptive to surroundings	✓				
24. is easy to transport	✓				
25. you like it!			✓		
Comments: Add up your ratings and get a total score:	76				

FIGURE 6.6

Situation 5. Game Idea Pops into Your Head—Bingo!
Introduction

Many years ago, I was planning a three-hour presentation on valuing diversity for a large group of employees at a big ten university. I knew the participants were coming from a broad range of occupations and backgrounds and would not know each other. I wanted an opening activity that would get them to mix and mingle and become aware of who all were present in the training. But it was a large group and I didn't want to spend a lot of time on the activity because I had a fair amount of content that I wanted to cover.

I had been working on a handout covering Loden and Rosener's primary (age, ethnicity, gender, race, sexual orientation, and physical abilities qualities) and secondary (education, income, religion, marital status, etc.) dimensions of diversity[3] and wondering how best to cover that material. Then, I switched back to worrying about an opening activity to get people acquainted. I had been to a training event a few weeks before then, where they had us play a game of "get acquainted bingo" in which we had to find people in the class who had different hobbies and experiences. I was considering doing something like that for the opening activity when the phrase "Diversity Bingo" literally popped into my head. I liked it. I could see it. The whole game filled my mind almost at once.

I sketched out a bingo card and started putting descriptors of various kinds of diversity into the squares. As I worked on the descriptors that went into the twenty-five squares on the bingo card, I began to realize the ramifications of what I was doing. I started writing out rules and guidelines for playing the game. I imagined the group playing the game and what would happen and the problems that would arise. I added more rules and guidelines and gave it a ten-minute playing time. I designed a Diversity Bingo card and made fifty copies.

I played the game at that presentation and it was a tremendous success, far more than I had expected. I rewrote, revised, and retested it. I asked my partner to help with the directions and additional information and resources that would eventually go into the packaging of the game. We decided that since this was a sensitive subject, the game packet would need considerable information on the various diversity characteristics and on how to play the game. I also included a few other games and activities that made use of the Diversity Bingo cards. We put it on the marketplace and have been selling it ever since. We have updated the materials two or three times, but the basic game and the basic Diversity Bingo card has stayed the same for almost ten years!

Diversity Bingo[4] is a highly interactive, experiential activity game. It was designed to raise awareness of the perceptions and assumptions that exist in regard to different dimensions of diversity. Because it is based on the familiar game of bingo, participants play the game and enjoy it. However, as the game progresses, some participants become aware of the difficulties of determining certain categories of diversity. Other participants become aware of ways in which they are "seen" or categorized by others. Almost all participants become aware of their own discomfort with some of the categories on the bingo card. Insights and discomforts experienced during the game are fairly minimal; and, because it is a game, people usually handle their discomfort with humor or avoidance.

But because it is an experiential game and one that deals with very sensitive subject matter, it must be carefully introduced, managed, and thoroughly debriefed. The first time I used this game in the situation I described earlier, I spent thirty minutes introducing and managing it, and an hour and a half debriefing it. The debrief was exhausting to the trainer and I realized that it was literally enlightening to many of the players. I was extremely fortunate that the initial playing of this game went so well. If I had not known the subject matter as well as I did and was not as familiar with and comfortable with the players as I was, it could have just as easily presented me with endless problems.

Game 5: Diversity Bingo

Summary: This is an experiential learning game that raises awareness of the perceptions and assumptions that exist in regard to different dimensions of diversity. Each player uses a Diversity Bingo card with twenty-five squares. Each square contains a descriptor of some dimension of diversity. The players mix and mingle and get the squares on their cards signed by people who match the descriptors. Players are given ten minutes to obtain a bingo and when they do so, they go to the facilitator to receive a prize. Any number of players can get a bingo.

Time: Thirty to ninety minutes depending on length of the debriefing.

Players: Any number can play.

Equipment: One Diversity Bingo playing card for each player; pencils and pens for players who might need them; enough prizes for each player to receive one if necessary!

Before and After Playing This Game

Because this is an experiential game, and one that involves very sensitive material, it is imperative that you be very familiar with the categories on the bingo card and very comfortable with discussing those categories. Read all the information on the categories that comes with the game and do further reading if you feel that you need to. Your own comfort in discussing the descriptors and the sensitive issues that will come up in this game is very important. Participants will look to you to model appropriate behaviors and appropriate ways of handling conflicting opinions as they arise.

Before the game, make sure that you have Diversity Bingo cards for all players, a good supply of extra pencils and pens, and some type of prize for all the players who get a bingo. I use multi-flavored rolls of candies for prizes because they are diverse and can be shared. You will want to prepare overhead transparencies or flip chart pages for the debrief and have them ready.

A large open space is needed to play the game most effectively. If there is enough space at the back of the classroom, use that; or, since the actual playing of the game only takes ten to fifteen minutes, you can take the class into the hallway, or into another room, or even outside if you need to. When the game is finished, reconvene the group elsewhere for the debrief. Also, since it can be lengthy, it is best to have the players seated for the debrief.

Introducing the Game

Introduce the game in a positive, upbeat manner, but be thorough in presenting the directions. Go through the rules carefully giving examples and illustrations whenever possible. Introduce the game before having the participants move to the area where the game will take place. Do not pass out the Diversity Bingo cards until just before the game begins. In fact, it works well if you lead the group to the game-playing area, then turn and distribute the bingo cards as they enter the area. When everyone is there and has a card and a pen or pencil, look at your watch, say "You have ten minutes to get a bingo. Anyone who gets a bingo within that ten minutes is a winner. When you get a bingo, show me your card and receive your prize! Let's see if everybody can be a winner! Ready, go!" Then stand back and let them play!

Managing the Game

Once the game begins, find a comfortable place for yourself on the outside of the group, but in a spot where you can monitor what's happening. You may want to take a few notes to use later in the debrief. If you gather some really great quotes and have the time, write them on a transparency to share with the class during the debrief.

When people come to you with a bingo, give them a prize and ask them to go back into the group so that more people can ask them to sign their bingo cards. You can give a two-minute warning if you like; and, if for some reason they are slow in obtaining bingos, you can give them a couple of extra minutes. When their time is up, call out "stop," and ask them to rearrange themselves in the debriefing area.

Debriefing the Game

Go through the debrief in a relaxed and reassuring manner. Have people think about the game for a minute or two before starting the discussion. You may want to start with "how do you feel?" before going over "what happened?" As the debrief unfolds, make sure everyone participates. Be certain to include, and if necessary, draw out the quiet players. It is important to keep the discussion to the point and moving along, but not hurried. Whenever possible, emphasize meaning and application of the learning more than just a repeating of what happened. Here is a standard set of debriefing questions modified for *Diversity Bingo:*

1. How Do You Feel?
   - About playing the game?
   - Frustrations, fears?

- Satisfactions, surprises?
- Other reactions?

2. What Happened?
   - How did you begin?
   - What began to happen after awhile?
   - What assumptions were made?
   - How were you perceived?
   - Strategies used?
   - Problems, difficulties, discomforts?

3. What Did You Learn?
   - About yourself?
   - About diversity?
   - Perceptions and assumptions?
   - Communication issues?
   - What else?

4. How Does This Relate?
   - To you and your life?
   - To your job, your workplace?
   - To our training purpose?

5. Where Do You Go from Here?
   - Applications?
   - Further information?
   - Comments, questions, concerns?

If you noticed certain interesting or unproductive behaviors being used during the game, and they are not mentioned by the participants during the debrief, share your observations with the group and ask them to comment. End by complimenting the group on the insights and comments shared in the debrief.

Assessing This Game

Using the Ultimate Training Game Assessment and the criteria that we established in Chapter 5, I would assess this game as shown in Figure 6.7.

Final Comments

Sometimes this game is almost too good. By that I mean that it can be very powerful and provide key learning moments that literally hang in the air for a long time after the game is over. I have used it enough now to periodically decide not to use it unless I will have the time and the situation to give it its due. It's not something to race through or use "just for an icebreaker." It needs time and depth. But when you give it the time and the depth, some powerful learning can occur.

What, So What, Now What?

This chapter has pulled together much of what has been presented in previous chapters. Hopefully, you have gathered some useful information about training games and how to use them in all of these chapters. The time has now come for you to apply this knowledge, which is why the next chapter is entitled, *It's Your Turn*. Good luck!

The Ultimate Training Game Assessment
Game assessed: Diversity Bingo

Rate each item: 4 = excellent, 3 = good, 2 = fair, 1 = poor, 0 = awful

Value as a Game:	4	3	2	1	0
1. fits with content, design, objectives	✓				
2. is challenging and engaging	✓				
3. adds variety and energy	✓				
4. has objective, measurable results	✓				
5. yields worthwhile amounts of learning	✓				
6. has suitable strategy for winning	✓				
7. works with various numbers of players	✓				
8. has a high fun factor	✓				
Learning Issues:					
9. repeats and reinforces key learning	✓				
10. gives immediate feedback		✓			
11. provides safe practice of new skills	✓				
12. develops understanding of concepts	✓				
13. provides meaningful challenge		✓			
14. stimulates many senses	✓				
15. promotes intense dialogue, discussion	✓				
16. provides social contact, group work	✓				
17. has realistic, complex experiences			✓		
18. has analysis, interpretation, reflection	✓				
Trainer Friendly:					
19. has minimal advance preparation		✓			
20. fits time, space, and cost constraints	✓				
21. fits trainer competencies	✓				
22. is flexible and adaptable		✓			
23. is nondisruptive to surroundings	✓				
24. is easy to transport	✓				
25. you like it!	✓				
Comments: Add up your ratings and get a total score:	**94**				

FIGURE 6.7

In a Nutshell

Games appear in training for a variety of reasons and to solve a variety of problems. This chapter takes you through five situations in which a training game has been designed: to solve a particular problem in the design or implementation of an established program; to make an activity into a game; to meet a key learning objective in a new program; as a means of getting prework done for a program; and when an idea for a game just pops into your head! The criteria listed in the Ultimate Training Game Assessment are used to guide the design and development of the games, as are the basic guidelines for what to do before and after a game and the information on how to introduce, manage, and debrief a game presented in Chapter 5.

Notes

1. Discovery Communications, <www.DiscoverySchool.com>, 2000.

2. Gayle Stuebe and Susan El-Shamy, *Card Games for Developing Teams* (London: Gower Publishing, and Amhurst, MA: HRD Press, 1999).

3. Marilyn Loden and Judy Rosener, *Workforce America! Managing Employee Diversity as a Vital Resource* (Homewood, IL: Business One Irwin, 1991).

4. Susan El-Shamy and Gayle Stuebe, *Diversity Bingo* (Bloomington, IN: Advancement Strategies, Inc., and San Francisco, CA: Pfieffer/Jossey-Bass, 1991).

My mother, my two sisters, my five-year-old daughter, and I sat around a plastic picnic table eating pizza in the Yogi Bear Pavillion of the Kings Island Amusement Park in Cincinnati, Ohio. This was my daughter's first trip to a theme park, and she was still reeling from all the options and possibilities. Looking around at us, she confided, "This is the happiest day of my life."

7

IT'S YOUR TURN

GETTING STARTED WITH TRAINING GAMES

By this time, selective perception has set in and you are probably noticing games everywhere. People playing games in the park. Game shows on TV. Training games listed in catalogs. And that's OK. Pay attention. Watch people play. In fact, make a point of watching trainers train with games. Observe your colleagues using training games. Take an e-course that uses games and see how you like them. If you can, go to a national training conference and attend as many sessions as possible that use training games. Watch the big names in action. Then, get busy and start using training games yourself.

To help you get started, this chapter presents guidelines for two important skills you will need: (1) changing activities into games and (2) creating your own games. You can begin with simple games and work your way up to longer, more complex games. You can start by changing existing activities into games, then move on to creating entirely new games of your own.

As you begin to design, keep a copy of the Ultimate Training Game Assessment nearby and periodically go through the three categories and the various criteria. Look at the basic guidelines for what to do before and after a game and the information on how to introduce, manage, and debrief a game presented in Chapter 5. Use the information and checklists to help you develop your training games.

1. Changing Activities into Games

As was mentioned earlier in the book, learning activities have many of the same effective qualities as games. They can engage the learner, present content effectively, and reinforce learning. A good activity will have a purpose, a set procedure, rules or guidelines and will often be followed by a debriefing session. But the competitive element is missing, along with some type of scoring that leads to winning and losing. The "fantasy world" element is often missing as well.

The first step in changing an activity into a game is to find an appropriate activity. Look for an activity that works well, but comes at a time in the program where more energy and vitality would be helpful. Midafternoon or right before lunch are time slots that come to mind. The activity should not necessarily be lengthened or made more complicated—just turned into a game.

It helps to keep the definition of a training game in mind: A training game is a competitive activity played according to rules within a given context, where players meet a challenge in their attempt to accomplish a goal and win, and in which the skills required and competencies being built in the game are those that are applicable beyond the game itself to the particular subject matter being studied. So, you will need to:

1. add competition,
2. change guidelines into rules,
3. give a context and a time limit,
4. make it challenging,
5. be clear about what constitutes a win, and
6. be sure the behaviors being practiced are applicable to course content.

The activity you are changing into a game should already be focused on behaviors that are applicable to the course content. To add a competitive element, look for a way to add a scoring component to the activity and stress the time limits. This may simply be a matter of stating how much time they have to complete the activity and that the first person or group to finish will win a prize. If the activity is a long one and has a few steps involved, you can impose time limits for each step and award points for completing them on time.

In fact, finding methods of awarding points can help change any activity into a competition. How do you do that? Well, let's see. You can award points for the following:

- for completing a task within a given time limit
- for being the first to complete the task
- for each criteria met
- for each right answer

Judges can be used to award points or present prizes. Participants themselves can be used to award points. One technique that I have used many times, I call "Vote by Dot." The final products from a participant activity are hung on the wall or laid out on a table or exhibited in some way. Each participant is given three round peel-off color-coding labels and asked to review the various "exhibits." They are to put a dot on or next to the three products that they consider to be the best. The product with the most dots wins.

Add or stress rules for the game, perhaps making them clearer or tighter than they were in the activity. Instead of saying that they have thirty minutes for the activity, you say that they have exactly thirty minutes to complete the assignment and that you will give them a five-minute warning. Add challenge by introducing special conditions or taking away some normal condition. For example, top off instructions for the game by giving them the extra challenge of carrying out the entire activity nonverbally with one point being subtracted for each instance of speaking. Extra challenge or special conditions can be justified by pointing out that in real life there are often unexpected circumstances that make carrying out ordinary tasks quite difficult.

Let's look at an example of changing an activity into a game. Say, for instance, that you are using a discussion activity that asks participants to go through a list of eighteen critical health or injury incident situations and determine which situations fall under which of four emergency procedure categories. The purpose is to practice making quick but accurate judgments regarding measures to be taken in emergencies. This is usually done by small discussion groups that have a half an hour or so to discuss the situations and assign them to a category. When the time is up, the instructor leads the entire group through a review of the situations and has them share and compare what categories they have placed each situation in and why. Such an activity can be interesting and could be used to practice skills, identify gaps in knowledge, and/or review particular material. But the activity is not exactly captivating or dynamic. And it really isn't what you would term "fun."

So, take the same activity, and divide the group into teams and tell each team to pretend that they are "Emergency Central," a command center for assigning emergency help and rescue teams. Tell them that they have only thirty minutes in which to assign eighteen situations to the most appropriate of four help and rescue teams according to the specific criteria that they have been studying. Add to that the existence of prizes for each team with a perfect score.

Add extra drama by bringing in a flashing red light, or a countdown clock that loudly ticks the minutes away. Make it difficult for each group to see or know what the other groups are doing. Hang large charts on the walls that list criteria for the four emergency procedure categories. Extra challenge can be added by incorporating unexpected additional tasks. With only five minutes to go, give them "three extra emergencies." Or add extra challenge by taking away something. Halfway through the activity remove the criteria charts from the walls. Introduce and monitor the game with a sense of urgency.

Points could be awarded for each right category assignment with bonus points for first team done and extra points for accurately assigning the final "three extra emergencies." Teams that accurately assign all or a specified number of the situations win a basic prize and perhaps a bonus prize could be given to the team with the most points. Prizes for this activity could be "medals" for a job well done—pins or stickers that say "good job." Chocolate medallions also work well.

And so, with relatively minor changes and a little extra fantasy and drama, a good training activity can become an exciting, engaging training game. Just because the subject matter is serious doesn't make using a game inappropriate. In fact, the more important it is that the learners really learn the subject matter, the more effective it is to use a game to reinforce and solidify that learning.

Your Turn

Just for practice, do some quick brainstorming about how you would change the following activities into games. Take a pencil and paper and write an A at the top left-hand side of the paper, a B on the left-middle side, and put a C on the left-hand side toward the bottom. Give yourself five minutes for each activity described below and quickly jot down as many ideas as you can about how you could change them into training games. What types of games would you choose? How would you include competition, scoring and measuring, and time limits? What about an element of fantasy? Write any and all ideas down and see what you can come up with!

A. What Is Creativity?

This activity involves participants reading through a dozen different definitions of creativity taken from various books, articles, and authorities and choosing the definition that they like the most and saying why they chose that particular definition. After participants have shared and discussed the various definitions and their choices in small groups, they write out their own "ideal definitions" of creativity and those are combined into a final class ultimate definition of creativity. The purpose of the activity is to get the group thinking and talking about creativity, what it is, what it means to them, and how it is generally viewed. The activity is the first major activity in a creativity workshop. It follows a rather uncreative introduction of the participants, the instructor, and the course objectives.

B. Career Options Exercise

This activity takes place in a career development class and follows an excellent video by Beverly Kaye called *Up is Not the Only Way.*[1] The participants are asked to take the six career direction options presented in the video—up, over, out, down, explore, and grow in place—and consider their own options in each of the six areas. Basically, participants fill out a form and then discuss their options with a partner. The instructor then goes through the six options one-at-a-time letting participants discuss each and what alternatives they see for themselves.

C. Good Vibrations

This activity is a summary review activity in a course for engineers and technicians that presents techniques for handling vibration problems during product development. It is a paper-and-pencil testing activity in which a variety of typical vibration problems are listed and participants must indicate which techniques are most appropriate for which problems. The tests are taken individually and then discussed item by item by the whole group. If nothing else, the name of this activity, should inspire you to unlimited possibilities for creative games!

What Happened?

Look over your paper and the ideas you jotted down. How did you do? Were you able to think of games that you could create from these activities? You can do the same thing with your own training program activities. Brainstorming is a great way to begin. Once you have brainstormed some possibilities, take some of the possibilities that appeal to you the most and develop them.

Get a copy of the Ultimate Training Game Assessment and develop the game further, addressing as many of those factors as possible. For example, look for ways to immerse players in realistic, complex experiences (item number 17) by using real-world situations or following authentic steps or procedures. Make the game stimulating to the senses (item number 14) by incorporating colorful visuals, stimulating sounds, various movements, and touching and manipulating devices into the game along with verbal activities.

Once the basics of the game are fairly well developed in terms of what players will do and how they will do it, begin to think about how you would actually implement the game. What would be needed, and how long would it take? Using the checklist in Chapter 5 on Basics to Cover in Game Instructions, think through and then write out instructions for your new game. This will help you think of all aspects of the game.

Once you have the game fully developed, it's time to test it out and see how it goes! You can try it with friends and colleagues, or if the game has been a relatively simple expansion of the activity, you might go right into trying it out in a program. Test it, make whatever adjustments seems necessary, and use it time and again. You now have an involving training game that will help reinforce the learning in your program. And, once you have changed an activity into a game a time or two, chances are you're ready to create your own training game.

2. Creating Your Own Training Games

As we discussed in Chapter 6, games can appear in training in a variety of settings and are used for a variety of reasons. They may be part of the original design of a program or they may be added at a later time to solve a particular problem. Whatever your reason for creating a training game, you will want to be guided by the various criteria in our ultimate training game assessment form and you can use the guidelines for introducing a game to think through and write out the steps to your games. Now, let's go through step-by-step procedures for creating a word search game, a card game, and a board game. Why not take a try-as-you-go approach as you go through the following material? By the end of the chapter, you'll have the beginnings of some useable training games!

A. *Creating a Simple Word Search Game*

Word search games are easy to make, simple to use, and can give a boost of energy to any training event. Follow the steps below and see what kind of a word search game you can create.

1. Choose a topic. Think about the different training programs that you are delivering. Choose a topic that can provide a list of words—basic characteristics, key components, major factors, people, places, events, and such. Here are some examples:

   • characteristics of good leadership,

   • characteristics of good teamwork,

   • key components of superior service,

- major factors leading to workplace accidents,
- ten types of computer errors,
- twelve cities where company has offices,
- eight departments in your company, and
- top ten ingredients of a powerful presentation.

For example, if you were teaching a unit on environmental awareness and wanted to get participants thinking about the issues and topics that would be covered in the course, you could have a word list like this:

EARTH, OZONE, TOXIN, POLLUTION, ENERGY, WASTE, RECYCLE, REUSE

2. Make a few copies of a blank word search form.

3. Begin putting words into the blanks. Starting with the longest words, pencil them into place on the form. Make some go across, some down, others up, a few diagonal. Make some go forward and others backward. Work at this until all of the words have been entered.

4. Now, fill in the remaining blanks with other letters. Make sure you use a nice variety of letters and include all the letters of the alphabet. Try different arrangements. Make it as easy or as difficult as you like.

5. Make a final copy. When you have an arrangement that you like, make a final copy on your computer or by hand. If you use a PC, make a table in Microsoft Word and fill it in with letters. If you use a MAC, try a table in Microsoft Word or make a grid in QuarkXpress (see Figure 7.1).

6. Test it. Once you have a word search that you like, make a few copies and try it out with friends, family, or colleagues. If it's too easy or too difficult, work on it until you feel it is just right. Then make enough copies for your next class and try it out.

7. Don't give the words. Whether you use the word search to get a discussion started or to review basic concepts, don't give the participants the words to start with. Not having the words to

			E	L	C	Y	C	E	R
E	T	S	A	W				N	E
		O					O		U
			Z			I			S
	N	I	X	O	T			Y	E
				U	N			G	
			L			E		R	
		L						E	
	O							N	
P		H	T	R	A	E		E	

A	N	X	E	L	C	Y	C	E	R
E	T	S	A	W	O	Z	U	N	E
S	F	O	B	C	Y	V	O	M	U
B	X	F	Z	I	E	I	F	A	S
I	N	I	X	O	T	N	U	Y	E
D	R	M	G	U	N	C	M	G	B
I	W	T	L	E	L	E	G	R	L
Q	U	L	H	B	G	O	J	E	C
U	O	C	P	W	U	K	O	N	K
P	I	H	T	R	A	E	Z	E	E

FIGURE 7.1

look for makes it necessary for them to think about the topic, and to consider for themselves the qualities of effective feedback, or whatever the topic. Let them try to find the "eight" words or the amount of words you have. If they have trouble finding the words, you can give them the words later.

8. Make it a game. So far, what you have is an activity. Now, make it into a game. That means, add competition, rules, time limits,

and some type of story line if you can. Will participants do the word search in small groups, with a partner, or individually? How much time do they have? Do they need to find every possible word in order to win? Or is the first person done with all the words found the winner?

9. Use it! Play it in your program and see how it goes. You can make necessary changes as needed.

B. *Designing a Card Game*

Remember that card games are a particularly effective training device for practicing and refining participant knowledge of concepts and principles and for applying models, techniques, and approaches. Use the steps that follow and create a card game for one of your training programs.

1. Decide on content and purpose. Think about the different training programs that you are delivering. Choose content that can provide you with a list of characteristics, discussion situations, or strategies or techniques for doing something.

2. Decide on the type of cards. Choose from one of the following:

   • Characteristic cards. These give key characteristics of the subject. For example, the characteristics of a safe work environment or an effective team or a good catalog ordering form.

   • Facts or data cards. These contain information or questions about the subject matter. As an example, in a computer class on a particular desktop publishing program, a card deck could contain questions about how to accomplish various tasks in that particular program, such as "How do you create a table?" "How do you insert a picture?"

   • Situation cards. Different situations would be presented on these cards either for discussion and problem solving or for the practicing of new behaviors. For example, to practice handling customer complaints, a card deck could contain twenty example situations of common customer complaints.

- Strategies or technique cards. These would present various things to do in order to accomplish a particular goal. For example, they could give ways to improve meetings, techniques for process improvement, or strategies for selling automobiles!

- Multiple-choice questions. These cards each have a question with four possible answers on it. These can be used in one of two ways. First, you can put a question on the front of each card with four possible answers and put the right answer on the back of the card. But to do this, the cards must be kept in a box so that neither the questions nor the answers can be read before the appropriate time. Players pull out a card and read the question and choices out loud, give their answer, and then check the back of the card.

  A second type of multiple-choice card will have the question, the choices, and the answer all on the front of the card. But with this type of card, the opponent draws the card and quizzes the player. Both types work quite well.

3. List the possibilities. Make a list of possible characteristics, situations, techniques, or whatever you are considering. Try to come up with fifteen to twenty items. Now make a second list for another type of card, if you used characteristics for your first list, now try situations or techniques. Any subject matter that lends itself easily to a list of twenty or more items is a good candidate for your card deck.

4. Make a few test cards. Test two or three different types of card decks by trying them out. Once you have content for twenty or more cards, write the content on index cards. Sort through the cards and consider the possibilities for their use. Consider a variety of games and activities: discussion, card sorts, assessment, some type of implementation.

5. Try a few mock games or activities. Try playing with the cards and card decks. Arrange them in different ways on a table. See if they will sort into different categories.

- Try a discussion activity or game. Create two or three discussion questions: Why is this important? Is this something you need to do?

- Try a card-sorting game. Could you have a key question—Is this something our department need to improve?—and then sort the cards into three piles: yes, no, and maybe so?

- Consider an acting or artistic game. Could the cards be used to act out something? For example, could you pull a card and then draw a picture of something? Could posters be drawn to illustrate techniques or situations on the cards?

6. Decide on a game. Write a description of the game. Include the directions, rules, time limits, and so on. Decide on ways to make it challenging and engaging. Can you incorporate some type of story line?

7. Test the game. Test the game on family, friends, and/or colleagues. See how it works. Make note of what needs correcting or adjusting.

8. Make corrections and adjustments where needed.

9. Construct a final deck of cards. Make your final deck of cards by printing onto construction paper and cutting the paper into same-sized cards. If it looks good, make as many decks as you need for the game. There are also blank decks of cards available at most teacher supply stores that you can use. It is quite a task to write on the blank cards and they are too small for most printers, but you can print what you want on the cards onto clear adhesive labels and then press the labels onto the cards.

10. Use your card game; refine it; play it again and again!

After you have experienced success with one card game, try a second or third game. Then it will be time for you to move on in your training game design journey into the land of board games!

C. *Creating a Board Game*
Creating a board game is very similar to making a card game. In fact, you can follow steps one through four, up and through the develop-

ment of the card deck. Then you develop a game board and a game or two that can be used with the game board and the card deck.

1. Decide on content and purpose. Think about the different training programs that you are delivering. Choose a particular skill that you want to have practiced, or information that you want participants to consider, or maybe content that you want reviewed.

2. Decide on the type of cards. The content of the cards will be related to the purpose of the game. If you want to practice a particular skill, then situation cards might work well. If you are practicing the application of a concept, or model, or a process, then situation or strategy cards might be the best choice. If your purpose is to review data, facts, characteristics, or strategies, then those types of cards will work best. Multiple-choice question cards work well for a variety of purposes. Consider the card categories and information given in the Creating a Card Game section above and choose to produce characteristic cards, fact or data cards, situation cards, strategy or techniques cards, or perhaps multiple-choice question cards.

3. List the possibilities. Choose two or three types of cards and make a list of possible items to put on the cards. Try to come up with fifteen to twenty items. Imagine playing a game and drawing these cards. What would be expected of the player? Answer a question? Apply a model? Discuss the situation? Suggest an approach to solve the problem?

4. Make a test deck. Decide on one type of deck and write out fifteen or twenty test cards on index cards and play with them a bit.

5. How many players? Consider how many players you will use per game board. This will affect how many spaces you will need to get around the board. In general, the larger the board the more players it will accommodate and the more spaces that are required. However, the larger the board and the more players using it, the longer the game will take. So, if you do not want to use more than an hour for the game, it might be wise to use a

board that accommodates no more than four players and make as many boards and card decks as necessary.

6. Sketch out a few game board possibilities. Consider an 8½ by 11 size board with a simple pathway around the perimeter of the board. Or try a figure eight design. Or you might want to try a round pathway with crossing pathways across the diameter of the circle.

7. Make a test game board. When you find a game board design that you like, make a test copy of the board. This can be done in a number of ways. A basic game board can be designed on a computer using a desktop publishing and design program such as QuarkXpress. You can also put together a hand-drawn game board.

8. Decide how to determine forward movement. You will need to decide how movement around the board will be determined. Dice can be used or a spinner. These can be purchased at teacher supply stores or large discount stores. I have found the use of a single die most effective for small game boards that accommodate two to four players. Fewer spaces are needed and it's just easier to use the one die!

9. Determine the basic procedure of the game. Write out how the game will be played. Each player needs an object to move around the board. This can be a coin, a plastic pawn, or even a foil-wrapped chocolate! What does a player do when it is their turn? Draw a card and answer the question on it? If the player answers correctly, they move ahead the number of spaces on the die. Or, roll the die and move ahead that many spaces, then draw a card and discuss it with the group. Or, the cards could have numbers on them and you wouldn't need dice. A player could draw a card, answer the question on the card, and move that many spaces ahead. You could determine the number of spaces to move forward by the difficulty of the question on the card, the harder the question the more spaces forward.

10. Put it all together and try it out. Write out directions for the board game. Include rules, regulations, and what it takes to win. Use a couple of coins for moving objects, get a die, set the card

deck next to the test game board, and try things out. See how long it takes to get around the board. Imagine or act out three or four people playing the game, drawing cards, discussing answers, moving the game pieces around the board. How long do you estimate the game will take?

11. If everything seems to be working well, proceed to a pilot game. This means creating a full deck of cards. If you will have four people or less playing and it will take each person at least five and possibly eight rolls of the dice before someone reaches the finish line, then you will need at least thirty cards and maybe forty or more to be safe. If the most any one player can roll on any one turn is six, and you want each player to have at least four turns, then you will need at least thirty spaces.

12. Enhance the game board. Make a final game board to use for piloting the game. How can you enhance the game board and make it more fun? Consider a theme. Is there a theme or some type of motif that is part of the program itself? Is there a natural play on words or word association that is connected to the topic or content of the game? If no natural theme comes to mind, think about using a sports theme, or an entertainment TV show theme. Journey themes lend themselves well to game boards; you know, start to finish and the trip along the way! It could be a cruise, a hike, a safari, or a treasure hunt—whatever appeals to you and you think will appeal to the group. You don't want to get too carried away and have the theme overpower the purpose of the game, but an appropriate theme can add to the fantasy, other-world realm of a game.

You may also want to add "special spaces" on the game board. You can add a few chance spaces here and there and develop a small set of chance cards that make players move forward or back so many steps. Chance cards can be humorous and connected to the "theme" of the game board. Or you can just make a few of the spaces on the game board itself contain special instructions like "Bonus! Take five more steps forward!" or "Sorry! Move three steps back!" You can also make a couple of joker cards and when a player draws a joker, set it up so that they have to pay some type of penalty.

Add a fair amount of fun and challenge to the game. Consider the rules and the time factor. Find some type of appropriate prizes for the game. Consider how winners will be chosen: individuals or groups? those who finish first? those who finish within a time limit?

13. Test it. Once you have a board game that you like, try it out with friends, family, or colleagues. If it's too easy or too difficult, work on it until you feel it is just right.

14. Finalize the game board and the card deck. Once you have them the way you want them, make a few copies of each.

15. Use your board game with a class. Use it; refine it; play it again and again!

This is the type of board game that I have always used. There are other types of board games and other approaches to the design and development of board games. Steve Sugar has an excellent article in *The ASTD Handbook of Instructional Technology*[2] on adapting and producing a board game. His *Management 2000*[3] board game kit makes use of a bingo-style game board and Sugar also has a seven-step procedure to help you customize any board game with your own material that he presents in his book *Games That Teach*.[4] Thiagi has a flexible board game called *Stepping Stones*[5] and another board game that works with bipolar issues call *Extremes*.[6] All of these are frame games that allow you to use your own content.

Final Thoughts

Well, we've gone around the board together and we've almost reached home. By now you have probably learned more about training games than you ever needed to know and then some! I hope you've applied some of the information and techniques presented and begun using training games in your programs. They really do reinforce the learning. And if you haven't yet, I hope you begin designing your own training games. It can be a tremendously satisfying and creative endeavor.

There is one more part to this book. Chapter 8, which I've called "Games Galore", has lists of resources that will be helpful. I've put in an annotated list of training games that were presented in Chapter 3 and games that I have either used myself, played, or observed being used. Then there is a list of books of training games, followed by books about games, training, and training games. Finally, I've included a list of my favorite Web sites on games, training, training games, and related subjects.

As we come full circle in our journey together, let's end with one of the questions that we began with: What is there about playing a game that appeals to so many of us? Perhaps it *is* that combination of challenge and fantasy, that imaginary, closed world, defined by given boundaries and nonnegotiable rules, where we all begin as equal players on an even playing field, with the same amount of time and resources to accomplish the mission, or achieve the goal, and win. What better way to learn could there be? Learning doesn't have to be painful. Training doesn't have to be suffered through. Well-designed training games can reinforce learning and bring fun, energy, and involvement to your learning events. And that makes for exciting stuff!

In a Nutshell

This chapter presents guidelines for two important skills: changing activities into games and creating your own games. Use the information and checklists presented in Chapter 5 to help you develop your training games. To create a simple word search game choose a topic that can provide a list of words. Make a few copies of a blank word search form and begin putting words into the blanks, across, down, up, diagonal, forward, and backward, until all of the words have been entered. Fill the remaining blanks with other letters. Add competition, rules, time limits, and some type of story line if you can. Make a few copies and test it, refine it, and use it.

To design a card game, first decide on content and type of cards: characteristic, facts or data, situation, strategies or techniques, or multiple-choice questions cards. Then make fifteen or more "test cards" on index cards with the characteristics, situations, techniques, or whatever you are considering. Try a few mock games or activities using the test cards. Then decide on a game and write out a description including the directions, rules, time limits, and so forth, and test it. Refine the cards and the game and construct a final deck.

Creating a board game is very similar to making a card game. Develop a card deck and then develop a game board and a game or two that can be used with the game board and the card deck. Consider an 8½ by 11 board with a simple pathway around the perimeter. Use dice or a spinner. You will need to determine movement around the board. Write out directions for the board game including rules, regulations, and what it takes to win. Use coins or pawns for moving objects and proceed to a pilot game. Refine the game and the card deck, then enhance the game board with special spaces and a theme, for example, a cruise, a hike, a safari, a treasure hunt, or whatever appeals to you. Once you have everything the way you want it, make a few copies of each. Use it; refine it; play it again and again!

Notes

1. Beverly Kaye, *Up is Not the Only Way* (Irwindale, CA: Barr Films, 1993).

2. Steve Sugar, "Customizing a board game with your classroom material," *The ASTD Handbook of Instructional Technology* (New York: McGraw Hill, 1993).

3. Steve Sugar, *Management 2000* (Kensington, MD: The Game Group, 1989).

4. Steve Sugar, *Games That Teach* (San Francisco, CA: Jossey-Bass/Pfeiffer, 1998).

5. Sivasailam Thiagarajan, *Stepping Stones* (Bloomington, IN: Workshops by Thiagi, 1994).

6. Sivasailam Thiagarajan, *Extremes* (Bloomington, IN: Workshops by Thiagi, 1994).

I was in the Game Preserve hunting for a new jigsaw puzzle to have for the holidays when I observed two eight-year-olds walk into the store in awe. They stood in the middle of the room with their heads tilted back looking up at the endless shelves of board games rising to the ceiling. Turning around and around, they murmured, "Wow. Wow."

8

GAMES GALORE

RESOURCES, LIST OF GAMES, WEB SITES

This last chapter is a compendium of various resources in respect to training games. First is an annotated list of individual training games. This list includes the example games given in Chapter 3 plus a few favorite games that I have used or observed being used. Next, I've put together an annotated list of collections of training games. After that, you'll find a list of books about games, training, and training with games. These are all books that I have read, found useful, and keep on my shelves. I hope you find them helpful!

Finally, I've included an annotated list of my own favorite Web sites on games, training, training games, and related subjects. I know how quickly Web sites change and with the amount of "partnering, merging, and acquiring" going on in the realm of e-learning these days, I hope most of these sites are still there when you look them up!

Individual Training Games

BaFá BaFá by Garry Shirts

Type of Game: Experiential simulation

Number of Players: 12 to 35

Time Needed: 2 to 3 hours

Materials Needed: Director's kit and workbooks that come with the game

This is the classic cross-cultural simulation game in which participants come to understand the powerful effects that culture plays in every person's life. There is a fair amount of preparation involved, but it is a great game. It can be used to help participants prepare for living and working in another culture or to learn how to work with people from other departments, disciplines, genders, races, and ages. BaFá BaFá shakes participants out of thinking in stereotypes about anyone who is different. After an initial briefing, two cultures are created—Alpha culture, a relationship-oriented, high context culture and Beta culture, a highly competitive trading culture. Interactions between the two cultures lead to stereotyping, misperceptions, and misunderstandings that become grist for the debriefing. Available through Simulation Training Systems, Del Mar, CA. See www.stsintl.com.

BARNGA by Sivasailam Thiagarajan, with a manual by Barbara Steinwachs

Type of Game: Experiential simulation

Number of Players: 12 to 30

Time Needed: 2 to 3 hours

Materials Needed: One card deck per group, written instructions

This is one of my favorites! It is so simple, yet so powerful. In this experiential simulation game, participants learn to play a simple card game in small groups. When participants then begin to move to new groups for game playing, conflicts begin to occur. When players begin to discover that the rules are different in other groups, they undergo a mini "culture shock," similar to the actual shock experienced when entering a different culture. They then must struggle to understand and reconcile these differences to play the game effectively in their "cross-cultural" groups. Difficulties are magnified by the fact that players may not speak to each other but can communicate only through gestures or pictures. This game is available through Intercultural Press, Yarmouth, ME. See www.interculturalpress.com.

Build a Paper Plane by Jeff Stibbard

Type of Game: Content-focused or experiential construction game

Number of Players: Any number

Time Needed: 20 minutes

Materials Needed: Paper for making airplanes and some type of target

Participants make paper planes fly across the room and hit a target in this simple, flexible construction game. The activity can be an experiential actitivy used to illustrate the importance of testing and piloting or a content-focused game for practicing effective brainstorming. Stibbard gives variations of the activity that make it more gamelike, such as giving time limits, adding extra challenge by not allowing talking, and awarding prizes for hitting the target within the time limit. This is just one of fifty games in his book *Training Games . . .from the Inside* published by Business & Professional Publishing Pty Limited in Australia.

Caption Competition by Graham Roberts-Phelps

Type of Game: Content-focused flip chart game

Number of Players: Any number

Time Needed: 20 minutes

Materials Needed: Handouts, posters or flip chart pages with drawings or cartoons

Participants compete to create the funniest captions for pictures related to health and safety issues at work in this game from *Health and Safety Games for Trainers.* Of course, the main idea of the game lends itself to a variety of topics; all you have to do is find pictures or cartoon on your topic. As I mentioned in Chapter 3, I like to take pictures, cartoons, or humorous drawings and enlarge them on to poster-sized paper for ongoing competitions during workshops and programs. Participants can use sticky notes to write captions and post them under the drawings throughout the day. At the end of the day, some type of voting can be used to choose the winners for each poster. *Health and Safety Games for Trainers* is available through Gower Publications in the U.K. See www.gowerpub.com.

> *Diversity Bingo* by Susan El-Shamy and Gayle Stuebe
>
> *Type of Game:* Experiential activity game
>
> *Number of Players:* 12 or more
>
> *Time Needed:* 60 minutes or more
>
> *Materials Needed:* Diversity Bingo cards, pencils, prizes

Here it is. Based on the traditional game of bingo, the *Diversity Bingo* game is a great addition to any type of diversity training program. Using specially designed "bingo" cards, participants mix and mingle, trying get a bingo by covering five squares down, across, or diagonally. Squares are covered by having people who fit the characteristics of a category, sign for those categories. Sample categories include "a person over 60 years of age," "a single parent," "a person of Asian heritage," "a person who is a veteran," and so forth. The real learning in this game includes how it feels to be perceived so narrowly and how easily we make assumptions about one another. The game package has background information on all of the diversity categories on the game card, instructions for playing and debriefing the game, and other games and activities that can use the Diversity Bingo Cards. This game is available from Jossey-Bass/Pfieffer (www.pfieffer.com) or from Advancement Strategies, Inc. (www.actionpacks.com).

> *Friendly Feedback* by Susan El-Shamy
>
> *Type of Game:* Content-focused card game
>
> *Number of Players:* 4 to 30
>
> *Time Needed:* 60 minutes or more
>
> *Materials Needed:* One or more *Performance Improvement Packs*

This game, which is both trainer and trainee friendly, is a variation of a feedback practice activity in *An Instructor's Guide to Action Packs*. Each small group of participants gets a full deck of *Performance Improvement* cards or each receives a deck that has been "stacked." One-at-a-time, group members draw a card, read it aloud and have two minutes to verbally use the coaching model being taught in that class as if coaching the person in the situation on the card. If they accomplish this in two minutes or less, they get five points. If it takes more than two minutes, but they do accomplish it, they get three points. If they can't do it on their own, group members can help them and they get two points. The groups do their own scoring and have fifty minutes to draw cards and practice the model. When the time is up, any group with thirty or more points gets a prize and the group with the most points gets a bonus prize. This game and others like it can be very flexible and easily adapted to the program content or the unique training situation. This game and others can be found in *An Instructor's Guide to Action Packs*. See www.actionpacks.com.

Full-Page Ad by Susan El-Shamy and Gayle Stuebe

Type of Game: Content-focused artistic game

Number of Players: 4 to 30

Time Needed: 30 to 45 minutes

Materials Needed: Flip chart paper and collage-making materials

This game produces some great advertising! "Full-Page Ad" is one of forty games in *Card Games for Developing Service* and it makes a great summary activity for programs on customer service. It uses the *Service Interaction Cards,* which contain cards giving things to do for better service interactions and things not to do. The group is divided into smaller groups of three to four participants. Each small group is given a few cards, large sheets of flip chart paper and multicolored marker pens. They then have twenty minutes to choose one behavior from their cards and draw a "full-page ad" promoting that particular customer service behavior. At "showtime," groups tape their ads to the wall and present them to the whole group. A fun variation of this activity is to have participants create collage advertisements using colored paper, sticks and strings, buttons, paperclips, stickers of all sorts, and whatever else gets thrown in at the last minute. For information on *Card Games for Developing Service,* go to www.gowerpub.com.

> *Hidden Squares* from John Newstrom and Edward Scannell
>
> *Type of Game:* Content-focused paper-and-pencil game
>
> *Number of Players:* Any number
>
> *Time Needed:* 5 to 15 minutes
>
> *Materials Needed:* Flip chart, transparency, or handout with the drawing of a large square divided into smaller squares

See how many squares you can find in this well-known paper-and-pencil game. Participants are shown a square divided into smaller squares and asked to count the number of squares that they see. They report varying numbers of squares depending on whether they count only the squares that are immediately evident or "dig deeper" into the problem and count squares that are made up of groups of squares within the drawing. It's a classic and an excellent tool for introducing discussions around perception, expectations, and paradigms. *Games Trainers Play* is published by McGraw-Hill and is widely available.

> *Management 2000* by Steve Sugar
>
> *Type of Game:* Frame board game
>
> *Number of Players:* 2 individuals or 2 teams
>
> *Time Needed:* 30 to 60 minutes
>
> *Materials Needed:* Game board, question cards, and playing pieces are all provided

Steve Sugar uses a nifty, bingo-style game board in this frame game, which lends itself to almost any topic. The game is simple in its rules and play and it can provide a great deal of information to the players in a fun and involving way. To customize, simply create a set of short-answer questions on your topic, transfer the questions onto cards, shuffle, and play. This game is available through the Game Group. See www.gamegroup.com.

Meeting Simulation by Gayle Stuebe and Susan El-Shamy

Type of Game: Content-focused acting game

Number of Players: 4 to 30

Time Needed: 90 minutes

Materials Needed: Copies of agenda, one deck of *Cards for Developing Teams*

You may discover another John Cleese as your participants take assigned roles and act out this meeting game from *Cards Games for Developing Teams*. An agenda is used that reflects a ninety-minute meeting with twenty minutes devoted to each of the four sections of the *Cards for Developing Teams* (unity, communication, support, and performance) and ten minutes for summary and comments. People are assigned roles of meeting manager, section managers, attendees, and notetaker. The overall goal of the meeting is to choose the "most important characteristic" from each of the four sections of cards. Of course to do this, participants must really understand their cards and listen carefully in order to vote on the most important. Participants can exaggerate and vent some of their frustrations about meetings and still play the game and learn about the content! *Card Games for Developing Teams* is available through Gower Publications in England and HRD press in the U.S.

Patterns Poker by Joshua Kerievsky

Type of Game: Experiential simulation

Number of Players: 2 to 14

Time Needed: 2 to 3 hours

Materials Needed: Design Patterns playing cards, tokens, or chocolates

"I'll see your three chocolate kissess and raise you one caramel." This is a comment you might very well hear while observing Patterns Poker, a game designed to help programmers learn the subtle art of how to combine design patterns. The basic idea of Patterns Poker is to come up with great pattern combinations in order to tell a great story about them. Cards are dealt, players study their cards, players exchange cards, and then players invent stories about their cards. Stories can be about how a system, or a part of a system, is implemented using the patterns. Participants tell their stories and the group decides on the best story. There is betting along with the play, using poker chips or chocolate candies. For more information and great pictures of programmers playing Patterns Poker, go to *www.industriallogic.com* and click on the games section.

> *Quick Draw* by Creative Advantage
>
> *Type of Game:* Experiential simulation
>
> *Number of Players:* 6 or more
>
> *Time Needed:* 20 to 40 minutes
>
> *Materials Needed:* Flip chart paper and colored markers

Quick, fun, and enlightening! Working in pairs, players draw a picture one line at a time. One player starts by placing two small circles on a page to represent eyes. Players then alternate adding one line or feature, going as quickly as possible. When a player hesitates, the drawing is done. The players then title the drawing one letter at a time, again alternating and ending when one player hesitates. Each pair should do at least two drawings. You can then display the artwork for all to see. This activity is great for illustrating concepts such as sharing responsibility, embracing failure, not self-censoring, letting go, and sharing control. You can make it into a game by adding structure, enforcing time limits, and awarding prizes. For more information, visit www.creativeadvantage.com.

> *Quizo* by Steve Sugar
>
> *Type of Game:* Content-focused frame game
>
> *Number of Players:* 4 to 20
>
> *Time Needed:* 15 to 45 minutes
>
> *Materials Needed:* Game sheets, tiles, question cards—all provided in game

This bingo-style frame game can be customized with your own program material. You prepare and ask a series of questions on your program content and for every question answered correctly, players cover a space on the gamesheet. The game ends when a player covers five spaces in a row. Simple, effective, and great for content review. For more information, see www.gamegroup.com.

> *Running Blind* by Graham Roberts-Phelps
>
> *Type of Game:* Physical experiential
>
> *Number of Players:* 2 to 30
>
> *Time Needed:* 20–30 minutes
>
> *Materials Needed:* Jugs of water, glasses, blindfolds, a large room with chairs and tables

This short experiential game lets participants experience how much they rely on sight. It is a great way of driving home the message that wearing safety glasses in required areas is a good idea. The game has some participants leading other blindfolded participants through obstacles and finally carrying a glass of water. It's simple; it's easy; it's a little messy. But it's fun. This is one of many games in the book, *Health and Safety Games for Trainers,* published by Gower Publishing in the U.K. See www.gowerpub.com.

> *Safety Bingo* by Graham Roberts-Phelps
>
> *Type of Game:* paper-and-pencil matrix game
>
> *Number of Players:* 2 or more
>
> *Time Needed:* 15 to 30 minutes
>
> *Materials Needed:* Handouts with grid of 9 squares, small prizes

Graham Roberts-Phelps uses a simple nine-box matrix in this game of "Safety Bingo." First, participants choose nine numbers between one and twenty-five and place them anywhere in the grid. Then the instructor reads questions numbered one through twenty-five. When participants hear a question with one of their numbers, they write down the answer to that question in the appropriate square. Later the instructor reads the questions, solicits the right answers, and has participants grade their papers. All of those with five answers in a row win a prize! This is such a simple design, but it is quite effective. It can be used as an icebreaker to get things started in a fun way, as an "assessment" tool to ascertain knowledge gaps early in training, or as a summary activity at the end of a program. This is one of many games in the book *Health and Safety Games for Trainers* from Gower Publishing. See www.gowerpub.com.

The Sales Journey from The Lead Group International

Type of Game: Content-focused and experiential board game

Number of Players: 3 to 15 per game board

Time Needed: 2 to 6 hours

Materials Needed: Game boards, card decks, workbooks, guide-
   books—all are included

The Sales Journey is just one of the Lead Group International's great board games that are designed around a three-dimensional performance model covering head (analytical and technical expertise), heart (positive relationships), and courage (embracing change, taking risks, and taking action). This particular game develops relationship-selling skills, puts participants in the "customer's" shoes, and deals with learning to overcome roadblocks on the sales journey. This game can be a separate stand-alone training program or can be integrated into existing sales programs. *The Sales Journey* can be purchased from Lead Group International in Lilburn, Georgia. For more information, see www.leadgrp.com.

Star Power

Type of Game: Experiential simulation

Number of Players: 18 to 35

Time Needed: 2 to 3 hours

Materials Needed: Chips and instructions come with game

This provacative simulation game comes from the Simulation Training Systems people, who also produce BaFá BaFá. In *Star Power* participants are challenged to progress from one level of society to another by acquiring wealth through trading with others. The first two rounds are very sociable. People are laughing, talking, and having a good time exchanging chips. Then the wealthiest group gains power. Barriers spring up between the various levels of the society. Communication gets strained. The group that has the power often tries to protect their power through illegitimate means. The others respond by giving up, organizing, or overthrowing the power group. After the simulation winds down, participants discuss power in safe, yet revealing ways. It's a powerful game! For more information, check out www.stsintl.com.

Stranded in the Himalayas by Lorraine L. Ukens,

Type of Game: Experiential simulation

Number of Players: 5 to 8 per small group

Time Needed: 1 to 2 hours

Materials Needed: Player activity books, leader's manual

This involving simulation game, designed by Lorraine L. Ukens, was a great help to me not long ago when I was doing a course on consensus building. It uses the subject of survival in the Himalayas as an interesting way of introducing work teams or other groups to the concepts of consensus and synergy in decision making. The game provides group members with immediate feedback on how well they perform as a team. The leader's manual contains all the information that a leader or facilitator needs to conduct this simulation and the activity book contains the engaging simulation—every participant needs a copy. This game is available through Jossey-Bass/Pfeiffer; see www.pfeiffer.com.

Triangles by Sivasailam Thiagarajan

Type of Game: Experiential simulation frame game

Number of Players: 12 to 23

Time Needed: 1 to 2 hours

Materials Needed: Various instructions sheets, copies of a blueprint, several pairs of scissors

This interesting simulation game with a surprising twist explores factors associated with planning and implementing new work processes. It is designed around interactions among three-groups (such as managers, workers, and customers or designers, trainers, and learners). The game kit comes with information on how to modify the game to highlight other themes such as employee involvement and quality control. So, it can be used as an experiential simulation game on planning and implementing new processes or modified to address other situations. This game is available through HRD Press. For more information see www.hrdpress.com.

> *Where Is It?* by Elyssebeth Leigh and Jeff Kinder
>
> *Type of Game:* Experiential simulation
>
> *Number of Players:* 20
>
> *Time Needed:* 60 to 90 minutes
>
> *Materials Needed:* Lists of participants, maps, floor plans, lists of things to find, small prizes

Participants run around large areas such as factories, hotels, or hospitals trying to find items or get answers to questions in this game with a "treasure hunt" format. The goal is to increase their ability to navigate a large area that they will need to know well so that in the future they will be able describe it to others and give directions for locating specific destinations. The first person or group back to home base with all of the items or correct answers wins the game. This is one of forty games in *Learning through Fun and Games* published by McGraw-Hill Australia.

Books of Training Games

The Accelerated Learning Handbook: A Creative Guide to Designing and Delivering Faster, More Effective Training Programs

Dave Meier, McGraw-Hill Professional Publishing, New York, NY. If you are a Dave Meier fan, and I am, this is his great three-day workshop in a book and more. Accelerated learning is an approach to teaching and training that actively involves the whole person, using music, color, emotion, play, and creativity, as part of training. This book includes an overview of the background and underlying principles of accelerated learning, a review of how the latest brain research supports accelerated learning theory, and many examples of how it is being used in corporations to speed up training time, improve learning, and reduce costs. The book provides over 200 accelerated learning techniques that involve the emotions and all five senses of learners in the learning process.

The Big Book of Customer Service Training Games

Peggy Carlaw and Vasudha Kathleen Deming, McGraw-Hill, New York, NY. This "Big Book" contains fifty creative games and activities that teach customer service basics—treating customers with respect, listening well, smoothing out ruffled feathers, and other skills an employee needs to sell and serve customers. Designed for anyone who manages front-line service workers, the book is full of fun, engaging games. This big book is available through Amazon.com and other training material providers.

Card Games for Developing Teams

Gayle Stuebe and Susan El-Shamy, Gower Publishing in the U.K. and HRD Press in the U.S. This was Advancement Strategies' first compilation of card games on one topic. It has a card deck that can be used for assessment as well as games. *Card Games for Developing Teams* is a team development tool consisting of a series of games and activities designed around a deck of fifty-two "Developing Teams" cards. The cards present fifty-two behavioral characteristics of effective teams, divided equally into four key team skills: unity, communication, support, and performance. The thirty games in the collection include discussion games, card sorting and assessment games, acting and artistic games, as well as a number of games designed for use back in the workplace. This set of games is available from Gower Publishing in the U.K. (www.gowerpub.com) and from HRD Press in the U.S. (www.hrdpress.com).

Card Games for Developing Service

Gayle Stuebe and Susan El-Shamy, Gower Publishing, U.K. We went a bit overboard with this set of card games. Just couldn't stop thinking of more cards and more games! *Card Games for Developing Service* is a versatile learning resource consisting of forty games and activities for developing service effectiveness, designed around two unique decks of cards. The fifty-two Service Interaction Cards present behavioral characteristics for effective front-line customer or client service. The fifty-two Service Environment Cards present behaviors that support and encourage a service-focused culture. The forty games in the collection include discussion games, card sorting and assessment games, acting and artistic games, as well as games that focus on how to apply the behaviors directly at work. This game is available from Gower Publishing in the U.K. (www.gowerpub.com).

Games That Teach

Steve Sugar, Jossey-Bass/Pfeiffer, San Francisco, CA. Written for today's busy facilitator, this book offers over twenty flexible new designs plus insights on how to use them for your own training topic and audience. Even though the games are fun and involving, every game has a practical, instructional purpose—therefore, the title *Games That Teach*. The book also features the "Seven-Step Game Implementation Model," which guides you in customizing any game with your own material. Published by Jossey-Bass.

Games Trainers Play, More Games Trainers Play, and Still More Games Trainers Play

John Newstrom and Edward Scannell, McGraw-Hill, New York. This classic set of three books of exercises, activities, and games is advertised as being able to "help get any training session off the ground fast—or jumpstart one whenever it lags—with the more than 400 proven activities. Page after page of fun, easy-to-use exercises help you: break the ice and get participants acquainted; shake up outworn habits and perceptions; challenge with thought-provoking brainteasers; test learning and retention; develop communication and listening skills; bring out and involve participant-leaders; win back lethargic, distracted, low-energy groups; encourage creative problem-solving; boost or reinforce a group's self-image; forge cohesive work teams that value group effort; facilitate transfer of training to the job." Can't ask for more! Available at fine bookstores everywhere.

Health and Safety Games for Trainers

Graham Roberts-Phelps, Gower Publishing, U.K. Every aspect of health and safety at work is covered in this collection of nearly one hundred games, quizzes, and exercises, including: safety awareness; managing safely; office safety; first aid; display screen equipment; risk assessment; environmental awareness; safe manual handling; fire safety; personal protective equipment, and hazardous substances. The exercises are easy and simple to run. They focus on generic skills and knowledge, and are consequently ready-to-use or easily adapted to the specifics of your own organization. And all of them have been devised, developed, and tested by the author during safety skills training courses. See www.gowerpub.com.

The Instructor's Guide to Action Pack Learning Cards

Susan El-Shamy and Gayle Stuebe, Advancement Strategies, Inc., Bloomington, IN. This guide to Action Pack learning cards is filled with creative uses for all nine decks. Whether it's the Customer Service Cards, the Career Development Deck, the Leadership Development Deck, Quality Cards, the Performance Improvement Pack, the Survival Pack, the Super Sales Deck, the Team Development Deck, or the newly revised Diversity Deck, this small book is filled with games and activities. Included are warm-ups, icebreakers, discussion games and activities, card sorting and assessment games, acting activities, and more. Get more information at www.actionpacks.com.

Learning through Fun and Games

Elyssebeth Leigh and Jeff Kinder, McGraw-Hill, Australia. This is a unique collection of forty games and simulations for teaching such skills as critical thinking, communication, problem identification and solving, attitude change, and leadership. Each game is presented with information on audience, time, group size, resources, setting, setup, process, and debriefing. There is also some extremely good information on using games effectively. This collection is produced by McGraw-Hill Australia but is available at bookstores in the U.S.

Games by Thiagi — Simulation Games

Sivasailam Thiagarajan, HRD Press, Amherst, MA. All the simulation games in this collection by Sivasailam Thiagarajan reflect the real-world workplace and enable players to apply their new skills, concepts, and insights to their jobs. The games are especially useful in helping participants explore and practice new concepts and skills in a safe, nonthreatening context. Games included are Triangles, SH! Sexual Harassment, Cash Games, More Cash Games, Teamwork Games, Diversity, Simulation Games, and Creativity Games. See www.hrdpress.com.

Training Games — from the Inside

Jeff Stibbard, Business & Professional Publishing Pty Limited, Australia. This book is a great resource not only for some nifty training games, but also for information on the how, why, where, and when of using training games. Fifty different training games are presented complete with insider tips on how to use each game as a powerful training tool. The games cover topics like communication, change, leadership, goal setting, creativity, and teamwork.

Books about Games, Training, and Training with Games

Costello, Matthew J. 1991. *The Greatest Games of All Times.* New York: John Wiley and Sons.

Furjanic, Shelia, and Laurie Trotman. 2000. *Turning Training into Learning,* Shelia W. New York: American Management Association.

Gredler, Margaret. 1994. *Designing and Evaluating Games and Simulations*. Houston, TX: Gulf Publishing.

Jones, Ken. 1995. *Simulations: A Handbook for Teachers and Trainers*. London: Kogan-Page, and distributed in the U.S. by Stylus Publishing.

Lowe, Robert. 2000. *Improvisation, Inc.—Harnessing Spontaneity to Engage People and Groups*. San Francisco, CA: Jossey-Bass/Pfeiffer.

Milano, Michael, with Diane Ullius. 1998. *Designing Powerful Training*. San Francisco, CA: Jossey-Bass/Pfeiffer.

Millbower, Lenn. 2000. *Training with a Beat*. Sterling, VA: Stylus Publishing.

Noe, Raymond A. 1999. *Employee Training and Development*. New York: McGraw-Hill.

Parkin, Margaret. 1998. *Tales for Trainers*. London: Kogan Page, and distributed in the U.S. by Stylus Publishing.

Parlett, David. 1999. *The Oxford History of Board Games*. London: Oxford University Press.

Prensky, Marc. 2001. *Digital Game-Based Learning*. New York: McGraw-Hill.

My Favorite Training-Related Web Sites

www.actionpacks.com

This is Advancement Strategies Inc.'s Web site. It contains information about the Action Pack decks of discussion cards with sample games and activities given for each of the eight card decks. There is also information about Diversity Bingo and the Diversity Deck. You can also learn a bit more about my partner, Gayle Stuebe, and myself, if for some reason you would want to do that!

www.alcenter.com

This is the Web site of the Center for Accelerated Learning. Committed to accelerated learning methods and philosophies in training and education, the site has lots of tips, techniques, information, and examples of accelerated learning principles in action. There's also an excellent list of the guiding principles of accelerated learning. The Center itself offers workshops in accelerated learning and provides tools to help speed and enhance the design and delivery of training including accelerated learning materials, software, and other learning tools.

www.astd.org

This is the Web site for the American Society for Training and Development, the foremost professional association and leading resource on workplace learning and performance issues. ASTD has over 70,000 members in more than 100 countries and provides information, research, conferences, expositions, seminars, and publications. This is a great resource for what is happening in the field of training and development. It also has an excellent job listing service!

www.brandonhall.com

Brandon Hall is the author of the *Web-Based Training Cookbook* and various other electronic technology books and articles. His Web site offers well-researched information about e-learning. It's a good resource for trends, tools, and best practices and has lots of good links to other Web-based training sites!

www.click2learn.com

This is one of the leading new "learning portals" that describes itself as "a provider of people, products, and services to enable organizations to create, deliver, and manage e-Learning." They have different individual "learning centers" on all sorts of training topics that have articles, online courses, and other information. They also have free online trial courses. This is an interesting site—sort of the Amazon.com of e-learning.

www.cognitivearts.com

Cognitive Arts is Roger Shank's company that consults and designs interactive e-learning solutions. The company produces "Goal-Based Scenarios," a solution created by Roger Schank at Institute for the Learning Sciences. These simulated work environments let employees practice job skills, make inevitable mistakes, and receive mentoring and coaching from the organization's subject matter experts on a just-in-time basis. Sounds pretty neat.

www.creativeadvantage.com

Creative Advantage specializes in collaborative creativity. They have adapted hundreds of improvisational theater-based games and activities to the workplace. They call these activities "Juicers" and they are used to help achieve participation and improved results in meetings, training, and presentations. This site has some nice sample improv games. You can also buy a nifty set of cards called "Juicers."

www.designingwbt.com

The Designing WBT site is for trainers, instructional designers, and Web developers who want to create effective Web-based training. This site provides examples, demonstrations, articles, presentations, and material from the book *Designing Web-Based Training* written by William Horton. This is a valuable site and it has some great stuff!

www.digitalthink.com

DigitalThink is another one of the new "learning portals" that designs, develops, and deploys e-learning solutions to companies. It "offers course content that can be aligned with clients' business objectives and delivered on the Internet." They have off-the-shelf courseware, custom-tailored content, or anything in between. They also have one of those "take a free course" deals.

www.discoveryschool.com

A subsidiary of Discovery Communications Inc., discoveryschool.com says it is dedicated to making teaching and learning an exciting, rewarding adventure for students, teachers, and parents. It does provide some really great teaching materials for teachers, cool resources for students, and good learning products for parents. It has a lot of neat stuff that trainers can use. I love their puzzle-maker section.

www.elearningmag.com

This is the Web site for e-learning magazine. It is an online version of the magazine and an excellent resource for what's happening in the world of e-learning. I usually read the magazine immediately when it comes, then throw it away. Later when I want to refer to something in the magazine, I go to the Web site.

www.fastcompany.com

Fast Company is the Nintendo Generation business magazine. If you like the magazine, like I do, you'll like their Web site. Fastcompany.com defines itself as serving people's individual career needs with six custom-built Career Zones: Build Your Business, Lead Your Team, Go Solo, Reinvent Yourself, Launch Your Career, and Be a Change Agent.

www.funderstanding.com

This Web site offers information and research about trends and preferences for kids, 8 to 18. They offer state-of-the-art technology for data collection and data mining regarding kids. What I have found extremely useful is their section on Learning Theories.

www.games2train.com

Games2train.com stands out in corporate training for its Game-Based Learning approach, which it describes as "the ability to marry the fun of playing a video or computer game together with all the information needed to accomplish training objectives." They offer training solutions in the form of Internet/Intranet and CD-ROM-based training games and Internet /Intranet Game-Based Learning templates. They have some great demos that you can download and an excellent article on the "theoretical underpinnings" of their training approach.

www.growingupdigital.com

This site is dedicated to Don Tapscott's book, *Growing Up Digital,* and is designed as an online community for discussing the influence of technology on society and youth. Just like his book, this site is a great source of information for how young people perceive the Internet and other technologies. If you want to visit the minds of the future, this is the place to go. I particularly like the site's rules of "Netiquette."

www.horton.com

This is William Horton's Web site. Horton, the author of *Designing Web-Based Training,* is an expert on the productive and appropriate use of new media and communications technologies. This site has a nice list of game design and development links and all sorts of other helpful design material. Excellent resource for designers of e-learning.

www.interel.com

Interel produces a variety of action learning devices, including the electronic carpet maze that I have used in training programs for years. Each of their learning devices can produce a variety of learning environments that reflect group dynamics ranging from simple to complex. They can be used for developing leadership, coaching skills, creating high performance teams, and many other applications.

www.learningcircuits.com

Learning Circuits is ASTD's online magazine about e-learning. It presents feature articles, departments, columns, and peer interaction opportunities that help the reader better understand workplace electronic learning. This is a good online e-learning magazine.

www.learningware.com

LearningWare produces computer software for classroom or self-directed game show style learning games. These are involving quiz show type games and can add a lot of pizzazz to training programs. This Web site has downloadable demos!

www.Lguide.com

Lguide.com rates and reviews online courses. I really like their comparative reviews of different courses on the same topics; it's very well done. This is a good place for information on specific courses and they also have articles and research on e-learning.

www.linezine.com

This is the thinking trainer's online quarterly e-magazine with stimulating commentary on learning, performance, and knowledge in the new economy. It has features and dialogues and interaction opportunities. When I read the *LiNE Zine Manifesto* by Brook Manville and Marcia Conner, a challenging list of beliefs that they say will guide this publication, I said, "Wow!" and immediately bookmarked the site.

www.nasaga.org

The North American Simulation and Gaming Association (NASAGA) is a network of professionals working on the design, implementation, and evaluation of learning games and simulations. NASAGA's primary mission is to facilitate the use of simulations and games and to spread the principles and procedures of interactive, experiential approaches to education, training, management, problem solving and decision making. Nice people, nice games.

www.stsintl.com

This is the Web site of Simulation Training Systems, where you can find BaFá BaFá and other neat simulations on cross-cultural relations, diversity, empowerment, ethics, and sexual harassment for business and education. Not only are these excellent simulation games, they have great names like Pumping the Colors, Star Power, and What is No, and their packaging has really good graphic design!

www.thegamegroup.com

This is the Web site for Steve Sugar's company, The Game Group, which claims to "Turn Lead into Gold! by transforming dry, heavy-as-lead lessons into gold-en learning moments" through the use of games. You can get information about the Game Group and buy Sugars' Management 2000 board game and his Quizo game at this site.

www.thiagi.com

Leave it to Thiagi (Sivasailam Thiagarajan), experiential training's grand master, to have the most helpful, informative Web site there is for trainers. This site is full of freebies—free games, free puzzles, free software, free stories, articles, and handouts! And it has lots of tips for facilitating and instructional design. Plus, there is almost always some kind of e-mail game going on.

www.trainerswarehouse.com

Trainer's Warehouse is the place to go for all kinds of products designed to help trainers and presenters. Not only do they have bells and whistles, they've got easels and markers, badges and buttons, games and gags and travel bags. If you ever present in front of a group, this is the site to checkout. They also have a new section where trainers share information and ideas on how they have used various products in their training programs.

www.trainingsupersite.com

This is the Web site for Bill Communications/Lakewood Publications and all of their products, courses, conferences, magazines, and newsletters. Designed around the theme of a Training Mall, this site includes products from many suppliers, including HRD Press; a business lending library of videos and training programs; software demos and video previews. You can virtually browse and shop forever.

www.trainseek.com

TrainSeek.com is an e-commerce Web site designed exclusively for corporate trainers and other managers. You can find, preview, compare, and buy training products and services from literally thousands of vendors and hundreds of thousands of products, services, and seminars. As one of their vendors, I can attest to the great service they give to their vendors!

www.trainingzone.co.uk

This is the popular U.K. site for Training and HR. It has everything from training news, resources, courses, workshops, forums, surveys, and directories to partnerships and links to training publishers like Gower. They have a nice newsletter too, if you're interested. It's not only a good training information site, but it can give you a glimpse of what's happening in the U.K. training community. And I like to take a global glimpse now and then.

www.twitchspeed.com

This is the Web site built around Marc Prensky's book, *Digital Game-Based Learning*. Prensky hopes to make this site the main portal for all digital game-based learning, bringing together everyone in the field. That right there makes it a Web site worth keeping an eye on. There's also some interesting, neat stuff here!

www.wired.com

This is the online site for Wired magazine and it describes itself as the "premier service for news of the digital world." It provides a good overview of technology-oriented information and who is doing what in the e-world. I still prefer Wired magazine, mainly for its great design and page layouts, but this is a good online magazine. I go to it when my real copy of Wired is upstairs and I am downstairs, online and want to check something.

www.wrhambrecht.com

WR Hambrecht and Company is a financial services firm "committed to using the Internet and auction processes to provide openness, fairness and access for investors." I discovered this site when one of their analysts, Connie Ragan, was on a panel at ASTD. She was so bright and knowledgeable about e-learning that when she mentioned the reports available on their Web site, I took note and checked it out. I found an absorbing, insightful report on the e-learning sector of the economy. So, now, I check out the site every now and then just to see what's going on.

For Product Safety Concerns and Information please contact our EU
representative GPSR@taylorandfrancis.com
Taylor & Francis Verlag GmbH, Kaufingerstraße 24, 80331 München, Germany

www.ingramcontent.com/pod-product-compliance
Ingram Content Group UK Ltd.
Pitfield, Milton Keynes, MK11 3LW, UK
UKHW021431080625
459435UK00011B/232